Allah' God of the Moon

Why We Should Fear The Islamic Cult

By Steve Preston

2nd Edition

© Copyright 2014, Steve Preston All rights reserved.

No part of this book may be reproduced, stored in a retrieval system, or transmitted by any means, electronic, mechanical, photocopying, recording, or otherwise, without written permission from the author.

Table of Contents

INTRODUCTION..5
SHARIA LAW MADE SIMPLE 9
SHARIA IN AMERICA TODAY..12
JEWISH APE AND PRESIDENT OBAMA 16
STOP ISLAMATION 19
IS IT TACKING OVER?...20
PRESIDENT OBAMA'S MOSLEM SPEECH......................30
MARTYRS OF THE TWIN TOWER....................................32
CHRISTIANITY VERSUS ISLAM BASICS 35
WORSHIPING THE MOON GOD 39
CANAAN'S SEX CURSE 41
TOWER OF BABEL WAR 51
PHOENICIAN DESCRIPTION..54
EVIDENCE OF ELECTRICITY 57
3150BC SEMIRAMIS AND NIMROD..................................59
WHO IS ALLAH? 62
METEORITE WORSHIP...64
CRESCENT MOON SYMBOL..67
WAR MORE IMPORTANT THAN SEX? 71
MOHAMMED IS SUNNA 73
QURAN NOT THE MAIN BOOK 75
MISCONCEPTION ABOUT CHRISTIANITY......................76
CHRISTIAN GOD PREACHED LOVE OF ALL 83
ISLAMIC LAW 85
DOME OF THE ROCK FAKE ASCENSION......................87
MOSLEM SATAN 90
MURDER THE NEDA 92
KAFIR..94
HATE JEWS SUNNA..96
MURDER ALL KAFIRS 98
MURDER FOR LEAVING ISLAM 103
MURDER FOR NOT CONVERTING 105
SELF MURDER AND TERRORISM 107
ISLAMIC HEAVEN 109
JINNS..112

EL KARINEH AND THE JINN	115
HEAVEN FOR SODOMY?	117
ZODIAC CONFUSION	119
WOMEN GO TO HELL	121
DESCRIPTION OF HELL	123
CRIMES OF MUHAMMAD	125
CHILD MOSLESTING SUNNA	129
EXTERMINATION SUNNA	133
TERRORISM SUNNA	135
SUICIDE SUNNA	136
SEX SLAVE SUNNA	137
WOMEN INFERIORITY	139
WIFE BEATING	142
MORE WOMEN STUFF	148
FEMALE GENITAL MUTILATION	150
MURDER FOR DISHONOR	154
FLOG FOR FORNICATION EVEN TO DEATH	155
QURAN ENCOURAGES SLAVE SEX	156
ENCOURAGES SLAVERY	158
MOHAMMED SLAVE TRADER	160
FORCE RAPE IN FRONT OF HUSBANDS	162
WOMEN'S RIGHTS	164
RETALIATION MURDER	165
MURDER BY STONING	166
MURDER FOR NOT PRAYING	167
CASTRATION EXTERMINATION OF BLACKS	168
MURDER FOR PAYMENT	170
MURDER PRISONERS AND GAYS	171
LAWS OF JIHAD	172
CRAZY MUSIC LAWS	174
INNAPPROPRIATE LAWS	176
THE BLACK FLAG	177
WHAT ABOUT THE FUTURE?	180
CHRISTIANS LIVES UNDER MOSLEM CONTROL	181
SHIPTON'S MOSLEM WAR	183
JOHN'S MOSLEM WAR	186
NOSTRADAMUS' MOSLEM WAR	190
EZRA MOSLEM WAR	197
SIBYLLINE ORACLES MOSLEM WAR	200
MOSLEM REVELATION	202
CONCLUSION	204

Introduction

This book is about the horrors of the Islamic Cult. Some try to push it off as an actual religion of the Creator God, but very quickly one finds that its gross deception is not only bad, it is hugely dangerous with the following as the founding elements of the cult. Some of this text may seem hateful, but this is not my intent or feeling. This is written out of fear.

1. The worship of Yahweh of the Jewish faith should be thrown out and replaced by the worship of Allah' the ancient Moon God. He was the supreme god over 300 lesser gods that supposedly controlled the world for a time.
2. One should pray to the Meteorite in Mecca 5 times a day instead of a heavenly father.
3. One should kill all who won't believe that Allah' is more powerful than Yahweh.
4. One should blindly perform the commands of the prophet of the moon god, Mohammed. He is the Sunna of Allah; the perfect man 86 percent of the holy texts of Islam are simply showing how to live to emulate Mohammed.

5. One will get great reward for killing the Yahweh believers and that reward is amplified if one is killed in during the insanity.
6. The mark of the moon god [Crescent Moon] would be placed on top of worshipping places instead of any Godly image.
7. The Old Testament would be refused and substituted with vile sayings from Mohammed's Quran.
8. A man can only have 4 wives. He must say "I divorce you to one of them and then he can have another.
9. Wives must always look down and if they say no to sexual favor, the husband can whip her "lightly".
10. In death, Hell is mostly made up of women.
11. If a man is praying, he must stop if a woman passes or a pig.
12. If a Moslem does not kill an "unbeliever" he is an apostate and must be killed himself

I hope you can see this Islamic Cult is nowhere near, what one would believe to be a religion similar to a Christian concept. It is dangerous by its very nature. It is vicious, and it should be of great concern, especially with the recent control of the nation by one who professes its callings. Before we even begin, let's just look at a couple of verses of their Quran.

Quran 47: 3: Mohammed says "When you encounter the <u>unbelievers on the battlefield</u>, strike off their heads until you have crushed them completely; then bind the surviving prisoners tightly"

Quran 8:12: I will cast dread into the hearts of the unbelievers. Strike off their heads. Then strike off their fingertips"

These two verses can hold claim to the main teachings of this dangerous group.

1. The first sentence in no way is stating that the Moslems go around waging war where if one of the people they find is not a Moslem so they are required to harm him.
2. The battlefield is not about land or anything else, it is about Islam so these <u>Islamics are ALWAYS considering WAR</u>. So these statements are for ALWAYS.
3. Therefore, <u>if an Islamic sees an unbeliever and does not kill him, he is violating the law and deserves to die</u>.
4. An Islamic cannot simply win a battle, <u>he must continue until the evil is crushed</u>. [When I say evil, I am talking about the Evil against the evil which is the Christian "love thy neighbor" thing.
5. The Islamic must not just kill, <u>but also behead anyone not having the Moon God as their God</u>, not ready to kiss the meteorite, not ready to rape slaves and all the rest of the requirements of Islam.
6. After beheading, the <u>Islamic is to dismember the corps</u> to add to the deranged level of cultism. No telling what they are supposed to do with the fingertips.

I'm sorry I might have offended some of those who try to be Islamic without being Islamic. I know there are many that try not to hold to all of the Quran, but those people are endangering themselves as they are considered as apostates by the more avid Moslems and could very well be treated as an unbeliever.

There are several "codes'; in the treasury that makes up the laws of Islam. One is _"whom your right hands possess"_. That is code for slave or sex slave. *"Ape or Swine"* is code for Jewish or Christian. As we go through, I will try to highlight these things so you tell what it actually says.

IMPORTANT!!!

Additionally, we need to understand something VERY important. Anything stated in the first verses of the Quran that are negated in later chapters **never existed for the Islamic.** They are just pout there so they could point to an abstraction. I will show some of those as well. It would be funny if it wasn't so horrible.

1983-2013- Humanitarian groups estimate that since 1983, an estimated 2 million people have died from war and related famine in Sudan at the hands of the Islamic leaders. Anyone refusing to denounce Jesus and accept Islam is executed. Rape is used as a weapon.

Sharia Law Made Simple

This Sharia Law bit is misunderstood by many. Only 14% of it comes from the Quran while the remaining 86% comes from the example set by Mohammed as the Sunna [Perfect soul]. It sets up Muslims with religious and political guidelines for their journey on earth. We had better understand how dangerous this law is or we will find it seeping into our laws to show conformity, tolerance and political correctness which can ultimately destroy America. Of the most dangerous of the Sharia "LAWS" are the following. We will look at each as they ascribe to Mohammed's Sunna so we can better understand what they really mean.

Wife beating (Section m10.12)- Women are insignificant- *"A husband may hit her, but not in a way that injures her, meaning he may not break bones, wound her, or cause blood to flow."* [This is greatly amplified if the woman does horrible things like raising her eyes too high, not covering her face when others can see her, refused sex, flirts, or complains about extramarital sex.]

Murder for honor (Section o1.2)-One must live up to Mohammed's Sunna-*"The following are not subject to retaliation: a father or mother for killing their offspring, or offspring's offspring."*

Murder all apostates (Section o8.4) - No one can EVER leave Islamic Cultism-*"There is no indemnity for killing an apostate. Or any expiation, since it is killing someone who deserves to die."* – Think about this one knowing our President was a Muslim and possibly became a Christian. Someone kills him and the murderer is praised. This is one of the most horrendous laws possible. Even if people know the cult to be wrong there is too much fear to ever voice that opinion.

Murder all non Islamics- Obligation of Jihad (Section o9.1-o9.8) –This is not a maybe. This is a <u>MUST KILL</u> Law– *"Jihad is a communal obligation upon Muslims each year." "The caliph makes war upon Jews, Christians, and Zoroastrians until they become Muslim ----or else pay the non-Muslim poll tax."* I know it doesn't sound so bad. Just pay the Islamic overseers a tax and you can continue to have a non- Islamic country—IT DOESN"T WORK LIKE THAT!

Hate all non-Muslims (Quran 48:29) *"Those who follow [Muhammad] are ruthless to the unbelievers but merciful to one another."* Islam always distinguishes between Muslims and non-Muslims.

Commit Adultery or you won't go to Heaven- Because Mohammed [the perfect man] did it, it is required or you will not be perfect this includes- *Sex with multiple wives (m6.10), sex with slaves and captives (Quran 33:50), and sex with temporary wives (Quran 4:24).*

Steal-(Para. o14.6) - Sharia stealing laws include forcible seizure, snatching and running, and theft by betraying a trust or embezzlement. Corruption is rampant in Islamic states due to these exceptions.

Bear false witness- *"It is OK to break the intent of the oath, as long as you don't break the letter of the oath. (Tawriya) (Para. o19.1)* **and** *"When it is possible to achieve such an aim by lying but not by telling the truth, it is permissible to lie if attaining the goal is possible." (Taqiyya)* **Examples** *include protecting Islam or a Muslim. (Para. r8.2)*

If those sound like how you want America run, just continue to ignore what is happening.

Sharia in America Today

To appease the Islamic Cultism, We have done the following directly associated with disarming American right, liberties, and heritage:

Textbook Control-All textbooks in America must now be approved by Islamic councils that are controlled by the Muslim Brotherhood. If an offensive remark or one that could in any way be considered offensive, it is removed. [There is no Nazi council checking books to see if worship of Hitler is demeaned, but this worship of Mohammed is being pushed by the unseeing Americans.]

Colleges can no longer be critical of Islamic Insurgency- No course at the college level uses critical thinking in the history and doctrine of Islam. *"Under Sharia no aspect of Islam may be criticized."* If our children don't think there is anything wrong with Islam, they will have an easier time taking control.

Islamic Prayer Rooms- American employers and schools are met with demands for time and space to do Islamic prayer. Workplaces are being made Islamic worship sites through these special rooms and time off to pray. [To put this in perspective, there are no requirements for things like snake rooms for snake worshippers or areas where Nazis can worship their Hitler, but worshipping Mohammed's moon god is now forced into industry.]

Universities are asked to close swimming pools and other athletic facilities to be used for Muslim women. This expense is passed on to all students for the protection of Islamic radicalism in believing women are only to be used for sex.

Hospitals are being sued for not having Sharia compliant treatments.

Muslim charities give money to jihadists, as per Sharia law. They are being set up and allowed in our country out in the open. Skinhead charities, on the other hand worshipping Hitler are discouraged.

Muslim foot-baths are being installed in airport facilities, using tax money. This is in accordance with Sharia law.

Acceptance of the Islamic Adultery- Islamic "refugees" are allowed to bring <u>all of their wives</u> for welfare and medical treatment to America. Authorities will not act even when presented with evidence. Polygamy is pure Sharia--- OK! There are some weird Mormons as well..

Fighting for Sharia [Mohammed Worship] law-We are fighting wars in Iraq and Afghanistan to implement constitutions that have the supremacy of Sharia law as their first article.

Islamic Prayers in Congress-In June 1991, Siraj Wahaj, became the first Muslim to deliver the daily prayer in the U.S. House of Representatives. I'll bet he won't use the verse identified in this book. This prayerful Moslem served as a character witness for Omar Abdel Rahman in the trial that found him guilty of conspiracy to overthrow the government of the United States. More alarming still, the U.S. attorney for New York listed this same prayer giver as one of the "unindicted persons who may be alleged as co-conspirators" in the sheikh's case.

The FBI is systematically eliminating any counter-terrorism training material that focuses on Moslem. While this seems absurd, that is exactly what is happening. FBI instructional material about Muslims, which characterized them as prone to violence or terrorism, that the Prophet Mohammed was a "cult" leader; and that the more "devout" a Muslim was, the more likely he would be to commit a violent act. Absolutely all of these are correct and as you read this book, you will understand this exactly.

Moslem CIA Director-The last thing I'm going to mention here is just one of many appointees that are being looked at to change America into a Moslem State. In 2013, President Obama nominated an Islamic convert with a decades old connection to the most anti-American variant of that religion to a post no less potent than the **director of the CIA**. It has been brought out that John Brennan **has overseen,** approved, and encouraged others to bring known leaders of Hamas and the Muslim Brotherhood into the government in positions to advise the US Government on counterterrorism strategy. He has proven through his own comments publicly that he is clueless and grossly ignorant of Al Qaeda's strategy, and he converted to Islam when he served in an official capacity on behalf of the United States in Saudi Arabia. Additionally, he has substantial ties to high level Moslems in out country and in the Middle East. Of the huge threat of Islam, Brennan says. *"In Saudi Arabia, I saw how our Saudi partners fulfilled their duties as custodians of the two holy Mosques of Mecca and Medina. I marveled at the majesty of the Hajj, and the devotion of those who fulfill their duty as Muslims by making that pilgrimage."*

First Moslem or Moslem thinking President- Named Barry Soetoro he didn't think his name was Moslem enough and changed it back to Barak Hussein Obama and showed his feelings in college as presented next.

Jewish Ape and President Obama

To the Moslem, Jews are a special type of Kafir [evil unbeliever]. They think of them as apes or monkeys throughout their literature. Additionally, Christians were considered Swine. Here are a couple examples.

Quran 5:60 "Worse is he whom Allah has cursed and brought His wrath upon, and of whom <u>He made apes and swine</u>."

Quran 7:166. So when they exceeded the limits of what they were prohibited, we said to them: "<u>Be you monkeys, despised</u> and rejected."

Obama's Anti-Semitic Poetry

The United States President was brought up with this belief so he wrote a poem about the apes. Obama's Poem "Underground," compares Jews to fig-eating underwater apes and echoes Qur'anic verse. Let's investigate. The poem seems odd and sort of non-confrontational at first.

Under water grottos, caverns filled with <u>apes</u> that <u>eat figs</u>. <u>Stepping on the figs</u> that the <u>apes</u> eat, they crunch.

The apes howl, bare their fangs, dance,
Tumble in the rushing water,
Musty, wet pelts glistening in the blue.

OK! It might be about underground fig eating Apes, but submarine primates are rare and both apes and figs, are mentioned in the Quran. Anyway, a picture of the author is shown below.

Quran 95 says, "<u>I swear by the land of the fig</u> and olive [Palestine and Syria] and by Mount Sinai [Saudi Arabia], and by this secure land of the city of Makkah [Iraq] ----"

It seems that the poet believes that these warlike apes, the Jews of Israel, are exploiting, even despoiling the land in which they have settled. Note that the apes both "eat" the figs and are "stepping on" them. [Step on Palestine and Syria]

Now note that these apes [Jews] howl, bare their fangs [gestures of war], dance, tumble in the rushing water, musty, wet pelts glistening in the blue. Sounds like the Jews are pushed out and "tumble" into the glistening blue sea.

To make this clearer, here is what Isaiah 9:12 of the Bible had to say. "*The Syrians from the east and the Philistines from the west will bare their fangs and devour Israel.*" I don't know if Obama read this verse, but he surely wrote about it somehow.

With this new insight let's read the poem.

- Under water grottos, caverns filled with apes that eat figs. **[The evil world is now filled with Jews that have killed Moslem brothers.]**
- Stepping on the figs that the apes eat, they crunch. **[The Jews step on our Moslem brothers and they are crunched or crushed.]**
- The apes howl, bare their fangs, dance, **[Opposite to their Old Testament teachings, when the Jews engage in war and put up a fight--]**
- <u>Tumble</u> in the rushing water, musty, wet pelts glistening in the blue. **[They will be driven into the Sea will be killed by the Moslem brothers.]**

Possibly, he is just confused, but this does not sound like the "Moslem Apostate" he claims to be. One might think, his profession of Christianity is not sincere and he does not deserve to be executed as an apostate by his Moslem Brothers as required in their holy books. While our President tries to push Islamation forward, some are trying to hold off its insurgency.

Stop Islamation

Stop Islamation of America SIOA was founded in 2010 to halt the 13-story Muslim community center proposed for a location two blocks from the World Trade Center. Rather than sensing the danger, the Southern Poverty Law Center named SIOA an anti-Muslim hate group. The Anti-Defamation League also listed it as a hate group, saying that it "promotes a conspiratorial anti-Muslim agenda under the guise of fighting radical Islam" and "seeks to rouse public fears by consistently vilifying the Islamic faith and asserting the existence of an Islamic conspiracy to destroy 'American' values."

In 2011, Norwegian mass-murderer Anders Behring Breivik's anti-Muslim manifesto who quoted some of the SIOA in his writings so it was vilified further even though SIOA, the European counterpart, and Jihad Watch groups all condemned Breivik's attack.

In 2014, an anti-Israel ad by the *American Muslims for Palestine was allowed so SIOA countered with one showing the great affection* Hitler and the Grand Mufti had as the Moslems supported the Nazi dictator before and during World War II.

During this time, Attempts to show the Americans how dangerous this group is becoming has been thwarted by the unsuspecting, the anti-Jewish, and the anti-American groups.

Is It Tacking Over?

Fastest Growing

Islam the fastest growing religion in the world and now it is the fastest growing "religion" in America. Most major studies estimate a worldwide Muslim population for the year 2000 at roughly 1.25 billion people; that is, about one-fifth or 20 percent of the world's population. In comparison, all of the different sects of Christianity together are considered the largest religion in the world with about 33 percent of the world's population.

Where Are They?

In Europe it is estimated that the Moslem population doubled in 10 years with 2 million in Great Britain,5 million in France, 4 million in Germany, a million in both Netherlands and in Italy, an ½ a million in Spain. This growth comes primarily through immigration and a high birth rate. By 2025 it is believed it will be about 25% of the European population. One misconception we have about Muslims is that most of them are Arabic. While that is not exactly true, more than 68 percent of all Muslims live in Asia and more than 27 percent live in Africa. Indonesia has roughly 15 percent of the world's Muslim population. In South Asia almost one-fourth of the world's Muslim population live in Bangladesh, Pakistan, and India.

Moslems in America

High Muslim birth rate and immigration is the major increase in the US and Canada rather than conversion. Estimates of about 8 million practicing Moslems seem to be close with about a 25% increase in population over a 10 year period. The largest concentrations of Muslims are in California, New York, and Illinois, with an estimated 400,000 in the Chicago area alone, where our latest President is from. That being said, there are 2 population sectors that are starting to change that perspective.

Taking Control Form The Inside

In 1990- there were only about 50 Islamic schools in America. Today the number is over 200. Since about 1990 the number of "Registered Islamic Centers and Mosques" has tripled to "more than 2,500." In those schools and Mosques, the children are being taught to take control of the United States. Masudul Alam Choudhury, a Canadian Moslem professor of business, writes matter-of-factly and enthusiastically about the "Islamization agenda in North America." Muhammad Hisham Kabbani of the "Islamic Supreme Council of America" estimates that "extremists" have "taken over 80 percent of the mosques" in the United States. And not just the mosques: schools, youth groups, community centers, political organizations, professional associations, and commercial enterprises also tend to share a militant outlook, hostile to the prevailing order in the United States and advocating its replacement with an Islamic one. Additionally, there are growing concerns that there is an Islamic undertone taking control of our very government. Here are a few of the many examples.

1993-98-Abdurahman Alamoudi- Moslem Brotherhood member, who openly supported HAMAS, **became an advisor to President Bill Clinton and then-First Lady Hillary Clinton**. He was permitted to establish the Muslim Chaplain Program for the Department of Defense and then served as its nominating and certifying authority. Provided $20,000 in start-up funds for a Muslim

Brotherhood front organization" called the Islamic Free Market Institute. Much too late Alamoudi fell from grace, was arrested and imprisoned following conviction on terrorism-related charges as a senior al-Qaeda financier.

1996-Suhail Khan- Moslem Brotherhood Member was established by Alamoudi and appointed to the White House Office of Public Liaison, from which key position he was able to manage the access of the U.S. Muslim community to the White House.

1997- Khaled Saffuri, another Alamoudi pupil and Ikhwan Operative was put in as Alamoudi's deputy.

1998- Suhail Khan, vast Brotherhood connections, was appointed to the White House Office of Public Liaison, from which he was able to access of the U.S. Muslim community to the White House.

1998- Sami al-Arian, another Alamoudi pupil and Ikhwan Operative became another deputy. Eventually he was unmasked as a senior operative of the Palestinian Islamic Jihad and lost his position.

2006-2008-Hesham Islam became senior advisor for international affairs who worked for Deputy Defense Secretary Gordon England in the George W. Bush administration. He became point man for Pentagon outreach program to ISNA (Islamic Society of North America), an acknowledged affiliate of the Muslim Brotherhood. Hesham was named by the Justice Department in the summer of 2008 an unindicted co-conspirator in the Holy Land Foundation's HAMAS terror-funding trial.

2000-2003 Louay Safi held official positions with the Brotherhood-including ISNA and the International Institute for Islamic Thought (IIIT). As ISNA's Executive Director of Leadership Development, [He became the endorsing agent for the Pentagon's Muslim military chaplain program. He also served as IIIT's executive director (1995-97), and director of research (1999-2003) IIIT. Safi was named an unindicted co-conspirator in the 2003 trial of Sami al-Arian, who was convicted as a fundraiser for the terrorist group. NO matter, Safi was hired by the Pentagon under a Naval Postgraduate School contract to teach Islam to U.S. troops about to depart on deployments to Afghanistan. Safi was at Ft. Bliss on the day in November 2007 when Army Major Nidal Hassan gunned down thirteen service members and civilian employees. The Army Criminal Investigations Division subsequently opened an investigation into the Army's use of Safi to provide seminars on Islam -- and those seminars were ended. In early December 2011, Safi was permitted access to Ft. Hood in an attempt to present a check to them on behalf of ISNA. Safi's 2011 book, "Peace and the Limits of War" openly justified violence against apostates. In August 2011, Safi reappeared as a founding member and director of the political office of the Syrian National Council (SNC), a Syrian rebel group dominated by the Muslim Brotherhood

2011-12 On 19 October, an editorial appeared in the Los Angeles Times by Salam al-Marayati, president of the Muslim Public Affairs Council (MPAC) that threatened the

FBI to change all its training materials. By early 2012, it was reported that the FBI had "purged hundreds of bureau documents of instructional material about Muslims, some of which characterized them as prone to violence." The picture above shows our President taking his shoes off in reverence and bows to some more.

2012- General Martin E. Dempsey, Chairman of the Joint Chief of Staff, fired US Army LTC Matthew Dooley, as instructor at National Defense University, because he approved a course on Islam that identified the hostilities.

2006-2014 Rashad Hussain, is the Obama administration's envoy to the Organization of Islamic Cooperation (OIC). Hussain has close Muslim Brotherhood associations, including the American Muslim Council (founded by Alamoudi) and the IIIT. In his official capacity, Hussain is responsible for providing advice on national security and Muslim outreach. He assisted in writing the President's June 2009 Cairo speech, in which Obama announced a new approach to the Muslim world declaring war on President Hosni Mubarak. Hussain also acts as point man for the criminalization, internationally, of any criticism of Islam.

2007-2014 Eboo Patel, Obama Administration Advisory Council on Faith-Based Neighborhood Partnerships, spoke at a Muslim Students Association and ISNA convention, appearing on a panel alongside Tariq Ramadan, grandson of the Muslim Brotherhood's founder, and Siraj Wahhaj, who was named as a possible co-conspirator in the 1993

World Trade Center bombing and has defended the convicted WTC bombers. Wahhaj allegedly advocates the Islamic takeover of America.

2004- The 9/11 Commission Report contained hundreds of instances of the use of words like "Jihad," "Muslim," and "Islam,"

2008-by the time the FBI published its unclassified Counterterrorism Lexicon, those words were gone, entirely missing from the document.

2008- State Department, DHS, and the National Counter Terrorism Center (NCTC) all instructed their employees to refrain from using the words "jihad" or "mujahedeen" to describe Islamic terrorism and its perpetrators. A flurry of publications such as DHS's "Terminology to Define the Terrorists: Recommendations from American Muslims"

2009-National Intelligence Strategy- removed all negative Moslem words

2010- National Security Strategy – removed "jihad," "Muslim," "Islam," the "Muslim Brotherhood" or "shariah"

2012-Entire Executive Branch, including DHS and the Defense, Justice, and State Departments, of the U.S. government was busy purging all instructors and training curriculum that associated Islamic doctrine, law, and scriptures with Islamic terrorism.

1996-2013 Huma Abedin, first as Secretary of State Hillary's Intern and finally traveling Chief of Staff, she was a member of the MSA executive board. She was a MSA Executive Board member. She and members of her immediate family have been closely associated with top ranks of the Muslim Brotherhood, al-Qaeda financial support organizations, and the Saudi royal family, for instance, her mother, Dr. Saleha Abedin is a senior member of the Muslim Sisterhood. Still she is given full security clearance and responsibilities to advise the Secretary on Middle East policy and politics. **Abdullah Omar Nasseef** is another Abedin family member and **senior Muslim Brotherhood leadership figure and Saudi royal family insider with direct connections to financial entities implicated in pre-9/11 funding of al-Qaed**a. Secretary General of the Muslim World League MWL parent organization of International Islamic Relief Organization [IIRO], an al-Qaeda front tied to the 1993 World Trade Center and 1998 East Africa Embassy bombings. Nasseef and his financial organizations were listed as defendants in post-9/11 legal cases based on his involvement with Al-Baraka Investment and the Rabita Trust (listed by the UN Security Council for financing al-Qaeda.) **While being advisor to Hillary Clinton, Abedin and Nasseef** together, established Institute of Muslim Minority Affairs (IMMA) and were editors of its journal (JMMA).

2103-2014 Albedin continues as strong indications that the Clinton Center is a conduit for funneling money from the Muslim Brotherhood to the Hillary campaign which explains Huma Abedin being at the center of that campaign.

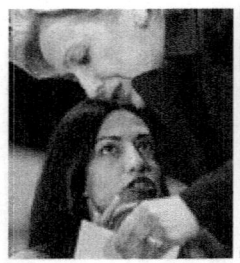

2013-2014- The attacks in Spain and in Bali and murders in the Netherlands and elsewhere have made the world realize that Islam is not just the enemy of America, but the enemy of the entire free world.

2012-2014 Mohamed Elibiary - a radical Muslim was promoted to a senior fellow position on the Department of Homeland Security Advisory Council. He is a vocal supporter of the Muslim Brotherhood. It is unimaginable that he has not been warned to keep his mouth shut or be removed from his influential position in the DHS. This shows the current administration will cater to the radical Muslim Brotherhood ahead of most non-Muslim groups. According to PJ Media, about a year after Elibiary's appointment, he downloaded files from the Texas Department of Public Safety and tried to sell them to a variety of liberal media outlets in an effort to defame Gov. Rick Perry but the media refused. In September 2013, he defended publicly Egypt's Muslim Brotherhood and claimed that all of the problems and violence was caused by the Christians. He failed to mention that Morsi had given all non-Muslims in Egypt three options: convert to Islam, pay a huge tax or leave the country. This was while Morsi's military was attacking Egypt's Christians, beating them, raping the women, looting their possessions and burning their homes and churches.

2010-2014 Islamic Society of North America (ISNA) was named, by the Justice Department as *an unindicted co-conspirator in the Holy Land Foundation terror funding case for its ties to the Moslem Brotherhood*. According to Frank Gaffney, the president of the Center for Security Policy, ISNA functions as a kind of umbrella for hundreds of offshoot Islamic Societies across North America. Yet, in spite of its DoJ status, this terror funding organization has been granted a coveted advisory role with the National Security Council (NSC) of the Obama White House.

2010-2014- Muhammad Magid, and ISNA's president, is not only the Director of the All-Dulles Area Muslim Society (ADAMS) Center, but also a member of the Department of Homeland Security (DHS) "Countering Violent Extremism" Advisory Council.

2009-2013- FBI Director Robert Mueller – *Very oddly* this man continues to defend CIA failure to take any action against Nidal Hasan, despite intercepting a series of emails between the *mass murderer and terrorist Anwar al-Awlaki, beginning as early as 2008.* In 2009, Hasan and al-Awlaki had communicated 10 to 20 times, mostly by email. Hasan's program directors at his fellowship and residency program ranked him in "the bottom 25 percent," that he was placed on "probation and remediation," and that he "often failed to meet basic job expectations". In June 2009, Hasan sent his last email to al-Awlaki regarding the perils that would befall any Muslim who failed to listen to Allah. On July, he was transferred to Fort Hood, and on November 5, 2009, he committed his atrocity killing American Soldiers.

2006-2013 John Brennen- As CIA station chief in Riyadh in the 1990s Brennen today holds the official title of Deputy National Security Advisor for Homeland Security and Counterterrorism. Former FBI Islam expert John Guandolo warned that the federal government was being infiltrated by members of the radical Muslim Brotherhood and this went to the CIA. Obama tried to appoint him as director of CIA, but now has backed off for a time under pressure from Congress. Mr. Brennan converted to Islam when he served in Saudi Arabia;" oddly "His conversion to Islam was the culmination of a counterintelligence operation against him to recruit him. --- Typically this happens is someone is a traitor or thought to be traitor material." Both seem to make him totally unfit for director of CIA.

September 2012- Benghazi Gun Running for Moslem Brotherhood- Of the 30 American Officials at the Special Mission Benghazi Compound that was attacked. It is believed 23 were CIA working out details of weapon transfer to Moslem Brotherhood soldiers fighting in Syria. After the Attack, Both the President and Secretary of State not only did not send aid, they lied about everything under the watchful eyes of Elibiary, Abedin, Hussein, Patel, Brennen, Magid, Mueller, Obama, and Clinton.

One way to hold off the onslaught of Islam is to present speeches about the danger.

President Obama's Moslem Speech

Those wishing to make Islam sound less awful always pick up the following verse.

Quran 5:32: "We decreed for the Children of Israel that <u>whosoever killeth a human being</u> for other than manslaughter or corruption in the earth, <u>it shall be as if he had killed all mankind, and whoso saveth the life of one, it shall be as if he had saved the life of all mankind.</u>"

In his speech on the loveliness of Islam, President Barrack Obama used this verse to show how great the Islamic religion really was. His version was almost identical. He said the following:

"Whosoever killeth a human being, it shall be as if he had killed all mankind, and whoso saveth the life of one, it shall be as if he had saved the life of all mankind."

This sounds so nice and sweet, it must be from one of the sweetest religions in the world, but let's look deeper. The Quran doesn't say the same thing. <u>He left out [for other than manslaughter OR CORRUPTION IN THE EARTH</u>. Of course, Corruption in the earth is saying corrupting the teachings of the only god Allah and Mohammed. If one does that, the killing is not only justified, <u>it is required</u>. That is

30

why over <u>300 million have been killed</u> by this barbaric "religion"

Quran 5:33 *:"The only reward of those who make war upon Allah and His messenger and <u>strive after corruption</u> in the land will be that <u>they will be killed</u> or crucified, or have their <u>hands and feet on alternate sides cut off</u>, or will be expelled out of the land. Such will be their degradation in the world, and in the Hereafter theirs will be an awful doom;"*

If the President wanted to show more about Islam, this would have been a more telling verse and it tells us what the corruption portion of the one he used meant.

Another way to show the efforts of Islamics taking our country is by building a mosque at the Twin Towers.

Martyrs of the Twin Tower

The On September 11, 2001 jihadists attacked and destroyed the World Trade Center. This was a requirement of Sharia law... *Quran 3:151:- Soon we cast terror into the Hearts of the unbelievers."*

Every year we hear about a monument to be placed near the world Trade Center destruction. While not specially identified, the monument will be built <u>to the 19 martyrs of Islam</u>. Millions of Muslims will travel yearly to New York to celebrate their great victory. One of the comments given is very telling. *<u>Let us build the greatest mosque the world has ever seen, with minarets soaring into the stratosphere taller then the demolished Trade Center</u> to show our good will and beg forgiveness for all the wrongs we have ever committed against Allah [the moon god].*

While this might sound like a voice of reason and an attempt at vilifying the animals that killed all those Americans, let's look at Sharia law again.

Sharia Law:--*Mocking anything in the Quran or the Sunna of the prophet Muhammad is apostasy and therefore punishable by death. Criticizing Islam, shariah law or the Sunna of the prophet Muhammad is apostasy and therefore punishable by death. Any Muslim who states a preference for democracy rather than shariah law or questions anything in the Quran or Sunna is a Kafir (disbeliever), considered an apostate, and therefore sentenced to death.*

There is no way these cultists want to deny the Jihadists their victory. They MUST try to expand awareness and praise the murderers or risk classification as an Apostate to be killed by the others…..

Quran 9:111: *"Allah hath purchased of the believers their persons and their goods; for theirs is the garden (of Paradise): they fight in His cause, and slay and are slain: a promise binding on Him in truth, through the Law, the Gospel, and the Quran: and who is more faithful to his covenant than Allah? Then rejoice in the bargain which ye have concluded: that is the achievement supreme."*

Muslim Jihadists rammed the twin towers in New York City and slaughtered 2,976 Americans to have access to a sex orgy in Heaven. They did the same in the London subway/bus massacres. They did the same in the Mumbai slaughter. Major Hasan did the same at Ft. Hood. With its offer of eternal erections and gratifying heavenly sex with virgins who "re-virginate" after sex, its little wonder Muslim terrorists, suicide bombers and other Islamic martyrs are dying to enter Islam's brothel paradise. I see no reason to give them a place to remember these "holy Martyrs". In fact, I don't consider them as martyrs at all. They are the lowest of low. Thugs trying to get a quick buck, or in this case a mass of women enslaved to them forever...

Christianity Versus Islam Basics

Let's see if there is ANY similarity between Christianity and Islam. I'm just going to bring up a few here as we will look at many as we go along.

While Jesus preached love *and kindness, Mohammed preached extermination, murder, slaughter, rape, terror, torture, hate, slavery, child molestation.*

Christians are sanctified *by the body and blood of Christ's own death and resurrection. Muslims are sanctified by the blood of murdered kafirs [all against Islam] guaranteeing accession to a virgin delight paradise.*

The Christian God is holy *and loving. The Islamic Moon God is a sexual pervert according to the claims set by Mohammed.*

Christianity can me defined by Loving *all including those who do you wrong. Islamic dogma pushes death and destruction to all who oppose.*

Christianity is marked with giving to the poor, *humbling oneself, and protecting children and women. Islamic goals include the debasement of all women, slavery, debauchery, suicide bombings, extermination, murder, war, terror, torture* and brutality against humans committed in the name of and to the greater glory of the moon God.

Christian teaching is to honor *one's wife.* Islam has the opposite women are property, degrading them is suggested, considering them inferior is required, forcing them to cover themselves against their will is common, beating is reasonable, sexual abuse is not bad, forcing marriage against their will is prescribed, girl child girls are allowed to be raped, and considering women as pigs is identified.

Christian belief allows slavery *but discourages it and gives rights to those enslaved.* Islam encourages and gives not rights to those enslaved.

Thou Shalt not Kill *is Christian.* Thou shalt kill in Islam.

Thou shalt not commit adultery *is Christian.* Only males are allowed to commit adultery including sex with slaves.

Thou shalt not have a God higher *than the Creator is Christian. Islam has the Moon God Allah and Mohammed.*

Thou shalt not make a graven image *is Christian.* Islam must pray to Mecca or be burned alive and kissing a holy meteorite is odd as well.

Thou shalt not claim you own words as God's *is Christian.* The entire Islamic cult is based on the debased Mohammed sayings professing to be from the Moon God.

Thou shalt not steal *is Christian.* Islamic men are allowed to steal another's virginity, life, and liberty.

Thou shalt not covet *is Christian.* Islamic ideals are to not only covet but take from those who are "lesser" or "unbelievers".

Christian Heaven is obtained by surrendering *ones self to love, faith, and belief in the death and resurrection of God Incarnate.* Islamic heaven is obtained by murder.

Christian heaven is love*.* Islamic heaven is lust and debauchery with erections that are constant and replacement of virgins to satisfy lust.

Christian law is equality*.* Islam law is superiority and extermination.

Christianity has prayer to God *as an act of reverence between a follower and his creator.* Islamics burn followers alive if they do not perform the required prayers at the right time. Because this was what Mohammed did and he is the Sunna [PREFECT MAN] anyone not burning a "late" prayer is violating God's Law and is threatened with HELL.

Christian law is humility*, sacrifice, and love.* Islamic law is war, murder, mass murder, killing, death and destruction, violence, terror, rape, unlimited sex with sex slaves, hate, violent jihad, terrorism, torture, brutality, savagery, maiming, beheading, wife beating, inferiority of women, honor killings, stoning, cutting off limbs, child sex, women as instruments of sexual pleasure in paradise, Sharia law, bigotry, intolerance, extortion, slavery, mutilations, looting, pillaging, sexual depravity, child molestation, oppression and subordination of women, inequality of kafirs, inequality of any human being, that kafirs can be murdered and their property stolen as a holy duty, that Muslims who renounce Islam can be killed, that Muslims (or anyone) who challenge the teachings of Islam should be murdered, that believers who slay and are slain in the service of God will ascend to a sexual Paradise of lustrous eyed, voluptuous breasted virgins who they can sexually molest for all eternity.

These two diverse concepts cannot be joined. They cannot be both tolerated or the strongest will win. When I say the strongest, I really mean the one that is more determined.

Moslems are going in number faster; they have more strictness in their religion, a tighter hold on their converts, and death to any who want to escape the worship of the Moon Goddess.

Worshiping the Moon God

A lot of Moslems will tell you they believe in the same loving creator God of the Christians; that Allah' is simply an Arabic pronunciation of Yahweh, but there can be no truth in it not only because of the direct opposition to all Jesus taught, but also because the Moon God never was Yahweh. Please look at all the flags of the Islamic nations before someone comes up to you and pretends that Allah' is the Arabic substituted word for name for either "Adoni Yahweh" or "Jehovah Elohiym", the 2 names for the Creator God. It is not! It is not! It all has to do with the Moon and that is why all the flags use the symbol of the Crescent Moon. Below is a collage of the various Islamic flags commemorating the Crescent Moon. While kissing a meteorite sounds like cultism, the reason is that their most powerful God is not the same as the Jewish and Christian Creator God is a lot more solidly defined.

Worship of Mohammed

While the moon God is important, the most important entity in Islam is Mohammed. Over 80% of the teachings of Islam are actually a study of Mohammed's SUNNA or his perfection with respect to what the moon God wants us to be like. Unfortunately, Mohammed loved sex, loved terrorizing, hated women as people, hated Jews and Christians, and hated all black people so to be like him means Islamic try to fill their lives with hatred and sex and they are told to lie, kill, steal, terrorize, and even become Martyrs to attain something close to his SUNNA and get rewarded with an endless orgy where your wife can watch you satisfy you lusts.

Speaking of sex, let's look at Canaan's Sex curse as sort of the beginning of this whole Islamic cultism. For the story, we will have to go back to the Son of Noah named Ham.

Canaan's Sex Curse

I think a general overview of how Allah' came about can help us understand why Islam got so twisted. We start right after the flood thing. Noah was drinking a little too much and his son Ham laughed at him. For some reason, Noah's grandson Canaan was "cursed" because of the laughter. There is a specific reason why Canaan was cursed and it was most likely not because his father, "Ham", saw his grandfather, "Noah", naked. It is strongly believed that, Canaan's curse was simply the last straw from a series of disrespect and other issues of Ham's son. Ancient texts tell us more about the incident than Genesis. Canaan and others in Noah's "Clan" had outside relations with "other people". I know you are thinking that Noah's immediate family was the only survivors of the flood, the Kangaroo in Australia was put their by someone from the Middle East, All the different races of people simply sprang into existence, and all people in the world were part of the CHOSEN ONES described by Enoch.

Well that is not the whole truth. Many texts explain that the ANAK [which means longheaded giants] and some of the Gentiles [those who were half-breeds] escaped the flood in various vehicles, but their bloodline was not pure. The ANAK, for instance had lost the capability to leave the Earth after death and would become demons and the Gentiles had a similar ending without something the Chosen Ones had [something the Bible calls the Light]. Anyway, I suppose you are wondering why I would bring up this strangeness, but please stay with me for a while. The only way the Chosen Ones could keep this {Light} was to keep a pure bloodline and never have children outside their group. 612 different "Laws of Separation" were adopted to try to keep the Jewish nation pure. In the end it was a failure but God Incarnate came along to put this {light} in the remaining "partial Chosen Ones] and the Gentiles, but I'm getting way ahead of myself.

Before we go on, let me tell you about the ANAK. They were giants, Lived for thousands of years, had capabilities obtained by their long lives, and they wanted to be worshipped as gods.

Canaan and the ANAK

Ham went outside his group and had Canaan. Noah was heartbroken and cursed Canaan with separation from God, but the outside marriages had already sealed their fate. Their descendants were no longer pure and they lost the comfort of being a "Chosen one". One of the offspring, of the outside union, was a man named Nimrod and that will bring us to Semiramis and eventually to the Moon God himself. For this review, I selected the book of Jasher, but others indicate similar details which will help us understand where this Moon God came from.

Nimrod's Mother Was Not from the Lineage of Noah

Jasher 7:23- And Cush the son of Ham, the son of Noah, took a wife in those days in his old age, and she bare a son, and they called his name Nimrod,

Other texts confirm that this second wife <u>was from the Gentiles</u>. We also find that Nimrod was extremely angry with God for killing off the Nephadim and many of the ANAK so we might assume that some of the descendants of the ANAK survived the flood. There is a strong possibility that Cush's second wife was one of them.

Noah's Clan Had to Fight the Others?

Jasher 7:31- And Nimrod strengthened himself, and he rose up from amongst his brethren, and he fought the battles of his brethren against all their enemies round about.

Of course all these enemies around the "Chosen Ones" were not Chosen Ones and if they were not, then they were not descended from Noah. The outsiders were of the ANAK also called Gentile. There was no question that God [I'm talking about the Creator God rather than the moon God] wanted the lineage of Adam to stay "sterile". Only the Adamics had something called the "Light" or heavenly spirit" that allowed them to go to heaven after death. The ANAK knew about this loss and tried desperately to regain this "light" by having children by the Adamics. This tactic did not work. It only made God angry.

People had Different Languages Before Babel

Jasher 7:45- And all nations and tongues heard of his fame, and they gathered themselves to him, and they bowed down to the earth, and they brought him offerings, and he became their lord and king, and they all dwelt with him in the city at Shinar, and Nimrod reigned in the Earth over all the sons of Noah, and they were all under his power and counsel.

You might wonder why all the people with different languages heard about Nimrod if they all spoke the same language. The answer is that they didn't speak the same language and they did speak the same language at the same time. The "voice" language was the one that only families could understand.

Below is the story of Canaan getting cursed?

Genesis 9:22-25-And Ham, the father of Canaan, saw the nakedness of his father, and told his two brethren without. And Shem and Japheth took a garment, and laid it upon both their shoulders, and went backward, and covered the nakedness of their father; and their faces were backward, and they saw not their father's nakedness. And Noah awoke from his wine, and knew what his younger son had done unto him. And he said, Cursed be Canaan; a servant of servants shall he be unto his brethren. [Canaan wasn't there when the naked incident occurred and none of his brothers or sisters were cursed. Only Canaan was singled out.]

Why Curse Canaan?

None of Canaan's brothers or sisters were cursed, nor was Ham, himself cursed. That might seem a little strange to you as it did to me. Well, I don't think that Canaan was singled out because he was the first one that came to mind. Try this on for size. The most likely reason for Canaan's curse was that he had already had sexual relations with one, or more, of the surviving ANAK or Anakim hybrids [Gentiles]. If you think I'm totally wrong here, what you must realize is that some type of action eventually caused the line of "demigods" that "popped up" throughout the country of Canaan and caused a tremendous amount of trouble. Part of that trouble involved one called Allah. The "naked" thing was probably an opportunity for Noah to identify his anger with Canaan. Of course, the Canaanites were not actually made servants of the world, as indicated in Noah's curse. At least they were not servants of normal people in the Middle Eastern world. These groups of "cursed" descendants of Noah were servants to the many ANAK giants that had controlling the region. Just think about it, if they weren't servants of the ANAK, whom did they serve?

Canaanite Giants

Later, the Canaanites split-up and mixed with the Philistinean and Egyptian, "red humans". They also mixed with many other groups that controlled the Middle Eastern lands. The land where they lived was eventually taken over by the Jewish refugees of Egypt, but before the Jews took control, the Biblical record indicates that, quite naturally, the rulers around the land of the Canaanites were giants. These giant rulers of Canaan were hybrid people, part ANAK, part human as discussed previously. The Jews thought of themselves as grasshoppers next to the mighty beings because the Canaanite rulers were so huge. The ANAK and Giants ruled the lands and the "more human" Canaanites were their servants, just as Noah had predicted.

Canaan Served the ANAK

For those of you that wish to stay away from religion, I'm sorry about all of this straight line Biblical historical track, but it is very important to trace the Adamics in all of this because of their special difference. You don't have to be aligned with any particular religious sect to believe the historical nature of the writings of ancient man, but learning the various historical elements of religious writings is a very important component to be considered. One such religious element is the man named Nimrod. The Nimrodian story leads us to the Tower of Babel. This tower is not known just to the ancient Israelites, but to people around the ancient world, so we can have cross-comparative reinforcement of the truth.

As I said before, Canaan didn't go with Ham on his journeys. We all have heard that Canaan's group began to spread out over the area known as Assyria and Canaan. The Bible, Sumerian accounts, Assyrian history, Greek Mythology, and Egyptian Hieroglyphics all indicate that the early kings of these regions were gods, demigods or ANAK. The rulers of the Canaanite lands were no exception. They also were humanoid gods.

One of Canaan's sons was named Nimrod or possibly Nimrod was the son of one of Canaan's siblings as suggested by Josephus in his history shown the following table. This Nimrod guy would have been one of the ANAK hybrids. He hated what God had done to the ANAK and publicly announced this animosity. With the help, or direction, of the ANAK, he then initiated what has been called the "Tower of Babel Heaven War". This was a third attempt at taking control of Heaven and, like the first 2, it was a failure, but while the war was going on, Nimrod gained control of the Middle East.

Genealogy of Noah's Kids

The following chart is a general genealogy taken from Josephus and other historians to sort of set in your mind how each of the players fit together in time. Most of the infiltration of ANAK blood is not shown, but notice that the Magog wife came from the lineage of Zeus according to ancient texts and Nimrod married into Noah's family and came from unknown hybrid parents. I need to get into some of the questioned parents that lead us to understanding the whole moon worship thing. I'm not claiming this to be completely accurate. I'm sure it is wrong in places, but it goes along with a great majority of the histories and shows the lineage for the Greeks, Irish, Canaanites, Persians, Babylonians, and Egyptians, so it is a reasonable tool.

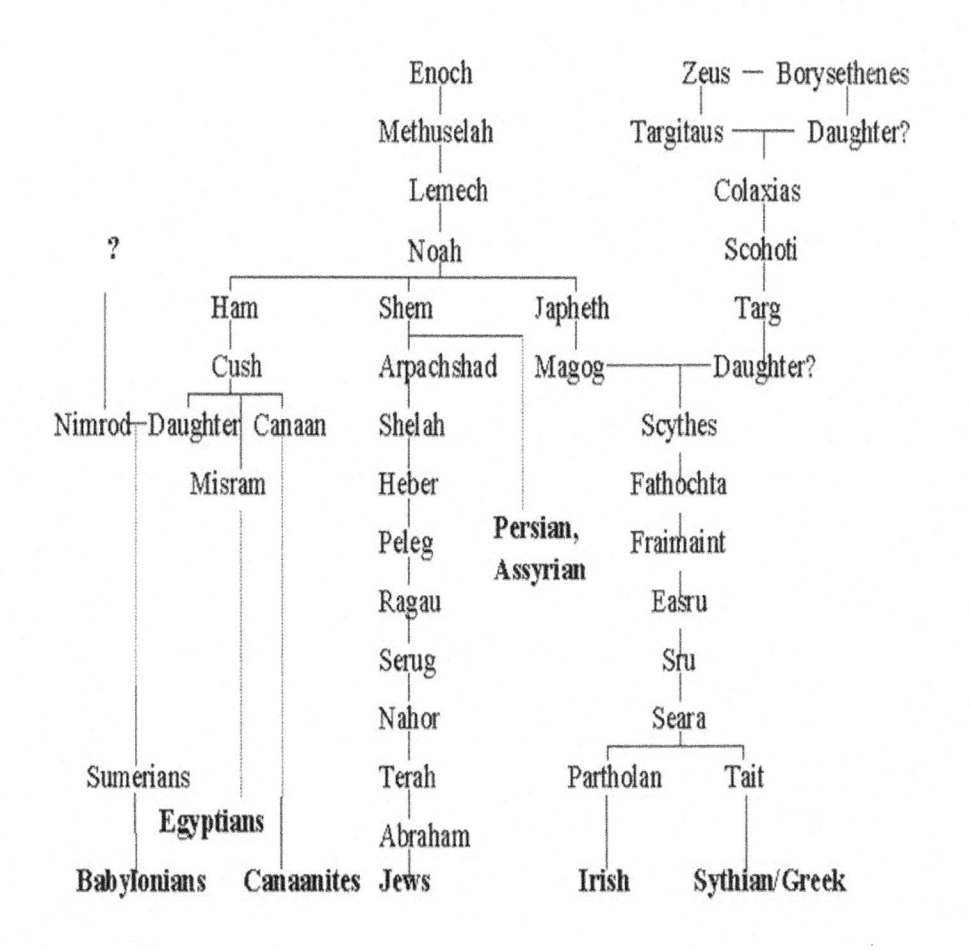

```
                        Enoch                Zeus ─ Borysethenes
                          │                         │
                       Methuselah          Targitaus ─── Daughter?
                          │                         │
                        Lemech                   Colaxias
                          │                         │
      ?                  Noah                    Scohoti
      │         ┌─────────┼─────────┐               │
     Ham       Shem              Japheth          Targ
      │         │                  │               │
    Cush    Arpachshad          Magog ──────── Daughter?
 ┌────┼────┐    │                                   │
Nimrod─Daughter Canaan  Shelah                   Scythes
      │                   │                         │
    Misram              Heber                    Fathochta
                          │          Persian,       │
                        Peleg        Assyrian     Fraimaint
                          │                         │
                        Ragau                     Easru
                          │                         │
                        Serug                      Sru
                          │                         │
                        Nahor                     Seara
                                               ┌───┴───┐
  Sumerians             Terah                Partholan  Tait
      │ Egyptians         │                     │        │
Babylonians Canaanites  Jews  Abraham          Irish   Sythian/Greek
```

Septuagint- And [Cush] begot Nimrod; he was a giant upon the earth. He was a giant hunter before the Lord God. [As we have seen, giantism was usually a sign of having ANAK blood, but there is more.]

Non-Adamic Lineage of Cush

Nimrod was from Cush, alright, but he was not a pure Adamic human by all accounts, so let's say Nimrod was hybridized.

I'll bet you thought the Bible indicated that Nimrod's father was Cush, but it doesn't really say that. The section of the Bible that doesn't say Cush was his father is shown below.

Genesis 10:6-12- *The sons of Ham: Cush, Egypt, Put, and Canaan. The sons of Cush: Seba, Havilah, Sabtah, Raamah, and Sabteca. The sons of Raamah: Sheba and Dedan. Cush became the father of Nimrod; he was the first on earth to be a mighty man. He was a mighty hunter before the LORD; therefore it is said, 'Like Nimrod a mighty hunter before the LORD.' The beginning of his kingdom was Babel, Erech, and Accad, all of them in the land of Shinar. From that land he went into Assyria, and built Nineveh, Rehoboth-ir, Calah, and Resen between Nineveh and Calah; that is the great city.*

1 Chronicles 1:9-10- *And the sons of Cush were Seba, and Havilah, and Sabta, and Raamah, and Sabtecha. And the sons of Raamah were Sheba, and Dedan. And Cush became the father of Nimrod: he became the first mighty man upon the earth. [Clearly Nimrod was not mentioned as one of Cush's 5 sons. He possibly married into the family. It is strongly believed that he was ANAK because of the indication of him being a mighty man just like the Genesis description of the Human/ANAK hybrids.]*

Jasher 7:3-*And Cush the son of Ham, the son of Noah, took a wife [This is not his Adamic wife that had the 5 sons listed in Genesis many years before this incident. It was a non-Adamic Hybrid woman.] In those days in his old age, and she bare a son and they called his name Nimrod. At that time the sons of men again began to rebel and transgress against God, and the child grew up. [The main transgression done by* *the people of this time was sex with the Demigods and ANAK. This transgressing is discussed in the same sentence as Cush's marriage for a reason.]*

Notice that **Nimrod was not one of Ham's sons**. He is not mentioned with the other sons and his entry into the family is specifically identified and a secondary event. Most likely, he simply married one of Ham's daughters, but the book of Jasher indicates that a secondary wife of Cush was the mother of Nimrod.

Here is an important point. The only way he could have gained so much power would have been through his non-Adamic side, because he was the 6th son of Cush and would not have a high place in the Cush family.

Notice that Nimrod was only the "first" to be a mighty man so there were many of his type in the old world;

Notice that the great city was either named Calah or Resen, not Babel.

Soon Nimrod took control away from his father Canaan who was married to another gentile named Semiramis.

Nimrod, King of the World

The ancient texts indicated that Nimrod defeated all the enemies of his brethren. Unfortunately, he worshiped the ANAK overlords. The texts below essentially say that the ANAK gods were vain and useless to the people who worshiped them. This sounds very close to the descriptions given by the Greeks when they described their gods.

Jasher 6:28-30- *And he rose up from amongst his brethren, and he fought the battles of his brethren against all their enemies. And Nimrod reigned in the earth over all the sons of Noah, and they were all under his power. Nimrod did not go in the ways of the Lord and he was more wicked than all the men that were before him.*

Jasher 8:15-20*- and that all their gods were vain and were of no avail. -- And King Nimrod reigned securely, and all the earth was under his control, and all the earth was of one tongue and words of union.*

Tower of Babel War

Before we get into how the Moon God got so much control and how Mohammed used the ancient beliefs to become one of the most powerful men in the region, we have a problem. Societies of that time were highly advanced. War destroyed that civilization and allowed the uncivilized people that remained to begin worshipping the ANAK and, after their death, images of the ANAK and their immediate descendants called ANAKIM or demi-gods. The war was centered around a massive citadel in Lebanon called Babel or Baalbek. The Baalbek name will make since as we go along.

Nimrod, Builder of the Tower

He is said to be the instigator, but I have to believe that the ANAK were behind the Tower of Babel thing. Josephus may give us insight into the ANAK involvement.

***Josephus**-Now it was Nimrod who excited them to such an affront and contempt of God. He was the grandson of Ham, the son of Noah. He would build a tower too high for the waters to be able to reach! And that he would avenge himself on God for destroying their forefathers [These were the ANAK and the Gentiles]. The multitude was very ready to follow the determination of Nimrod, and they built a tower.*

Nimrod was a Canaanite and part ANAK by all accounts. He hated what God had done to the ANAK.

The War Tower

There is no doubt that the Tower was made for War against Heaven. Exactly how it was to be used is a subject of great conjecture that is not important at this time. Here are various texts concerning the intent of the tower.

3 Baruch- These are the ones who built the tower and war against heaven, and the Lord removed them.

Ephtaem- If they waged war in height, how much more shall they conquer him whose warfare is on earth?

Day of Atonement- They built a tower and said, "Come let us split the firmament to make war against it." [Clearly, the Firmament here refers to planets although, with Mars and Venus destroyed by this time, I don't know which ones were worth fighting against.]

Jubilees Babel

The book of Jubilees chapter 10 provides us with another viewpoint. This set of verses not only tells us about the size of the building, it also gives us a glimpse into the reason it was built, and the war that followed. Brief details of this long lasting Babelic War will be discussed very shortly.

10:21-And they built it: 43 years were they building it; its breadth was 203 bricks, and the height [of each brick] was the third of one; its height amounted to 5433 cubits [2/3 meters] and 2 palms, and [one wall was] thirteen stades and of the other thirty stades. [See discussion that follows.]

10:22-And the Lord our God said unto us [God's trusted archangels]: Behold, they are one people, and this they begin to do, and now nothing will be withholden from them. Go to, let us go down and confound their language that they may not understand one another's speech, and they may be dispersed into cities and nations, and one purpose will no longer abide with them till the Day of Judgment.

10:23*-And the Lord descended, and we descended with him to see the city and the tower which the children of men had built. And he confounded their language, and they no longer understood one another's speech, and they ceased then to build the city and the tower. [While this Quran indicates that their speech was confounded, many others indicate that they could speak to family and close friends. In the next Quran note, the people could understand some and not others. The whole confounding/not confounding issue will make sense in a minute.]*

10:24*-For this reason the whole land of Shinar is called Babel, because the Lord did there confound all the language of the children of men, and from thence, they were dispersed into their cities, each according to his language and his nation. And the Lord sent a mighty wind against the tower and overthrew it upon the earth, and behold it was between Asshur and Babylon in the land of Shinar, and they called its name 'Overthrow'.*

Please notice that the tower WAS NOT IN BABYLON, but east of the land between Babylon and Asshur. It was probably in Baalbek, as no major cities exist between the two identified and shown.

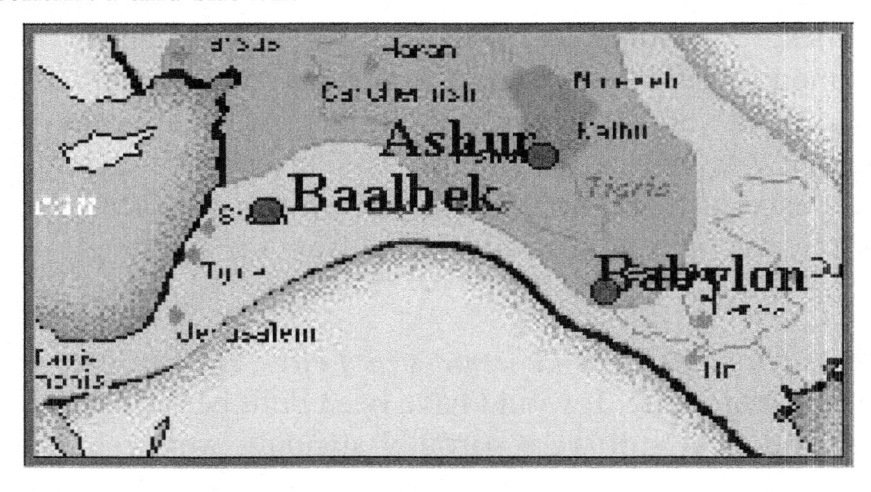

Phoenician Description

According to the book of Jasher, the war that followed was the worst ever witnessed since the flood. A third of the population around the world died outright and another third were deformed. Jasher indicated this group became like Apes. The remaining people had lost the ability to talk without using audible words and all were spread out around the world to begin a new civilization. The Ancient Egyptians called this time Zep-Tepi [A new beginning]. The Hindu called the new Age of Kali. The Mayan started there well known calendar----all at the same time 3150BC.

Babel and the Phoenicians

We have all heard the Jewish story about this place, but the Phoenicians had a very similar account. The Phoenicians may have told us a lot about the Tower of Babel being at Baalbek. Sanchoniatho wrote that Byblos [Baalbek] was Lebanon's first city and from his descriptions and descriptions of other ancient writers, it is evident that Baalbek was the site of the third assault on heaven. Here are some excerpts. The first statements are the historical record and the description following comes from the author.

Byblos [Baalbek] was Lebanon's first city- If Baalbek was the first major city. It would have been built before the flood. The cities that still were partially standing were rebuilt. In Peru and Egypt, the major cities were rebuilt; Atlantis was gone, before the flood and Baalbek was rebuilt. The huge boulders used kept much of Baalbek from being destroyed by the flood. It was a perfect base to start the attacks on heaven again.

Byblos was founded by Cronos- Cronos and the Biblical hunter, Nimrod, are closely paralleled. Nimrod is probably the demigod talked about here. According to other documents, Nimrod had made strong threats against God for destroying the ANAK with the flood and was going to get him back.

*Byblos was the grandson of Elioun-*This probably is reference to the Biblical Elohiym; however, Nimrod was the son of Canaan, Noah's cursed grandson. Both must be considered for reasonable interpretation. This probably is an indication that Nimrod was, indeed a hybrid.

*The demigods of Byblos possessed "Light ships"-*This statement indicates that there were many demi-gods or hybrids that survived the flood and worked with Nimrod in his eventual plan. The light ships were some form of flying ships the Sumerians called Merkaba.

*The father of Cronus devised Baetulia, contriving stones that moved as with having life.-*Here we are probably seeing some truth. The reason that huge stones were used in Baalbek's construction seems to indicate that its stones were levitated into place.

*Chief among the people was Taautus.-*The Egyptians called Taautus, Thoth. Being chief among the people indicates that Thoth was a demigod as evidenced in other ancient texts.

*Taautus who invented writing-*Ancient Egyptian texts talk about Thoth as the creator of the Egyptian language and he probably would have had that same task if he was in Baalbek.

Cronus was constantly at war with Elioun [Elohiym] and his father.-This probably is an account of the third war in heaven between the Nimrodian hordes and God. This war we sometimes call the "Tower of Babel War".

The auxiliaries of Cronus were the sons of Elioun-This certainly indicates that the ANAK were working with Nimrod to take over heaven.

Cronus gave all Egypt to Taautus that it might be his kingdom.

It seems that after the wars, the demigods lost and were dispersed, as indicated in the Biblical version. Thoth was sent to Egypt. He had been there before and was instrumental in building the great pyramid. Now he would be king. Cronos/Nimrod went to Babylon.

While the Citadel at Baalbek was completely destroyed, Babylon was still relatively livable so King Nimrod and his mother, soon to be wife went back to Babylon, the seat of the Sumerian empire.

Evidence of Electricity

Babylon was a modern, city during this time. Not only did they have running water, huge buildings, well laid out roadway, but they also had electricity. When I say electricity, I don't just mean stationary power, I also mean portable batteries. Details of Batteries during Zep-Tepi have been found in Egypt, India, Mexico, United States and Babylon, so we are not talking about completely backward societies.

Baghdad Batteries

The drawing on the right is one of several ancient batteries found in Baghdad. [A cut-away of the 2.5 to 3 inch jar shows the inside rod, the inner cylinder and where the wires were attached]. Guess what! More of these batteries were found.

After the initial find of a single battery, 4 more "batteries were found in a magician's hut in Seleucia and 10 more were evidently found at the some nearby site and placed on display in a German museum. It seems like these "D-cell" sized batteries were everywhere. The picture in the middle shows an actual Baghdad battery and a second one that is sliced open. A last picture shows the battery compared with a common D-cell. This "Baghdad Battery" contained something else equally interesting. The metal parts were put together with a substance that has been analyzed and determined to consist of 60 percent tin and 40 percent lead. Anyone in the manufacturing business knows that what they found on these parts was our present day mixture.

With this background, let's go to Babylon with Semiramis.

3150BC Semiramis and Nimrod

This queen was an odd one. Semiramis is the subject of many myths about her reign as both the wife and mother of kings. The one most known is Nimrod the builder of the Tower of Babel and one of the instigators of one of the worst wars in human history. Not did Semiramis become Nimrod's wife, she was also Nimrod's mother. She would have been the ANAK [Long headed Giant] or ANAKIM [Descendant of the ANAK] wife of Cush, his father.

Anyway, Semiramis and Nimrod began ruling Babylon together after the war. Nimrod was killed by a wild pig so she had him deified as the "God of the Sun". Then she became pregnant and had Tammuz who would be deified as well when his time came. Some legends have Semiramis as one of the ANAK who were an ancient race and Nimrod's power came from her as much as it did from his own power.

Nimrod had almost conquered the entire Middle East at one time, but melted at the sight of Semiramis, his mom. His prize may have been a big mistake in judgment. A 2nd mistake came when Semiramis, now Queen of Babylon, may have helped him get killed. Anyway! She had him deified as the Sun God, who had several names. The Main one we remember is Baal or Baalzibub. Anyway, this is where we get the name for Baalbek as I previously mentioned. Semiramis, when she died became deified as the Moon Goddess Ishtar who had fallen from the moon in a giant moon egg that fell into the Euphrates River. This was to have happened at the time of the first full moon after the spring equinox. Semiramis became known as "Ishtar" which is pronounced "Easter", and her moon egg became known as "Ishtar's" egg." Ishtar became pregnant and claimed that the rays of the sun-god Baal that caused her to conceive. Soon the Crescent moon of Ishtar was seen everywhere. Below is the image of Ishtar with a crescent moon above her head followed by Isis with her crescent moon at the base of the sun, and the Greek Artemis with a Crescent moon above her head. The 4th one is Luna Roman Goddess of the moon and the last is Selene Goddess of the moon in Greece. It can be easily seen that these are all the same person and the Moon goddess was not a male.

The religion had to change the sex or people would think they worshipped Ishtar and had Ishtar egg parties, and the Ishtar bunny. Well, it just so happens. Ishtar's son Tammuz died and was deified as well and he was considered the after death son of Nimrod or Baal. To get there we need to look a little deeper.

Who is Allah'?

Long before Islam, the Sabeans in Arabia worshipped the Moon God who was also known as Ilumquh. He was married to the Sun Goddess Dhat. I know this sounds backward but stay with me. They had three daughters -Allat, Aluzza and Almanat. These 3 deities where merged and they formed a triple goddess triad, like many other Moon Goddesses. It was this triad that would take on the entity of Semiramis/Isthar and Nimrod/Baal but this time the Moon would be a male having 3 daughters. Of these, the most common name was Allat. Soon Islamic tradition converted this triad into what was known as the <u>daughters of Allah'</u>. Allah's Daughters Allat, Manat & al Uzza ~ are all mentioned in the Quran 53:19. Their temples destroyed, when the Arabs were first forced upon pain of death to repeat the phrase 'There is no God but Allah', as Mohammed decided that having the women as powerful entities would not fit in his new "religion". The negation of the Daughters had begun.

Now Muslims agree that: "There is no god, but Allah and Mohammed is His messenger." More than a prophet, Mohammed was the epitome of their God. He is the "Sunna" of the moon God. He was the perfect soul, so to speak. To know Mohammed was to know Allah. He was the perfect God. In fact, there is much, much, more about Mohammed than the moon God in the trilogy of Holy books that make up Islam.

Islam Not From Ishmael

I know you are thinking The Moslems came from Ishmael as Abraham had the half-Egyptian son before having the Jewish one named Isaac. Because of that, you would think there should not be this bitter hatred between each other. Both children kept in touch throughout their lives and buried their father together, but the Jewish side inherited all things Jewish while Ishmael was told he would be farther of a great nation outside the Jewish line. Certainly, they would have initially held to some of the teachings of Abraham, but we must remember that there wasn't much in the way of "single creator" religion back then. As Ishmael wandered with his herds, he would have most assuredly attuned himself to the religions of the region with Baal and all the rest well before Mohammed came along. Whether he worshipped the sun God or the Moon God as the leader is not known, but he and the others of the region had many, many gods. Mohammed's father was even named after the Moon God well before Mohammed even came up with his new religion. That brings us to Meteorites.

Meteorite Worship

Like other cults, the Islamic Cultists worship a meteorite in the Dome of the Rock. "Meteorites-cults" are common in Greco-Roman civilizations. The Temple of Artemis at Ephesus contained a squat statue of the mother-goddess with a crescent moon on her head, carved from a meteorite that fell from Jupiter. The Palladium of Troy and the black stone or Baetyl in Emesa, Syria, are believed to be of meteoric origin as well. Likewise, the Phrygian mother goddess Cybele worshipped in Rome was a stone; most likely a meteorite. A further example is the meteorite of Pessinunt in Phrygia, which was worshipped as "the needle of Cybele," brought to Rome in a powerful procession after the Punic War on advice from the Delphic oracle. There the meteorite was worshipped as a fertility goddess for another 500 years." One Meteorite stone was worshipped along with Aphrodite. It is shown next to the left.

Muhammad took Mecca by force along with its most important possession of the gods which was its Kaaba [a big black meteorite] which had been in Messa for 700 years before Islam. Mohammed then did something Muslims continue to do today; he went over and kissed the Black Stone at the Kaaba, to worship it or the moon God it was associated with.

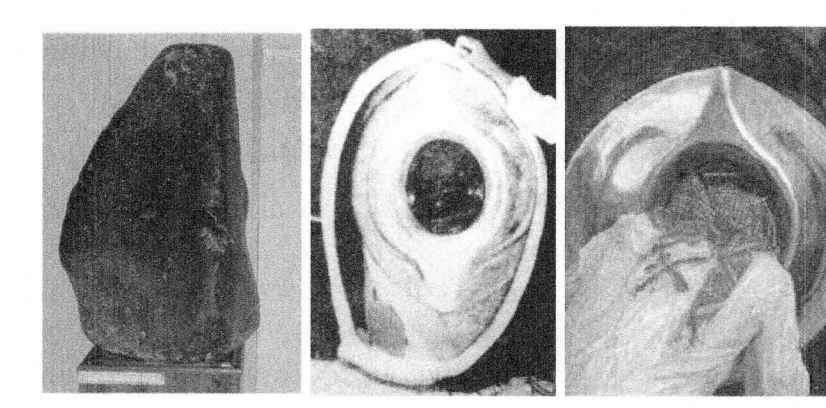

Islamic Allah Meteorite

Here is the important part of this story. Mohammed prided himself on taking no idols. But this stone was important enough to kiss. He did not think of it as an idol, because it represented what he believed to be the most powerful god of all the gods. Now his followers all continue to do the same. Once Mohammed took the Kaaba, he began the task of dismantling its Gods and Goddesses all except for one he would claim to be the supreme one, Allah. According to Mohammed, the meteorite is "Yamin Allah" (the right hand of God). It is a divine meteorite or "Bethel- Stone" predating creation. One story has it falling at the feet of Adam and Eve. It is presently embedded in the southeastern corner of the Kabah. The stone IDOL is worshipped by Islamics as a representation of the moon God.

Islamic Manat Meteorite

Don't think there are no other gods in the Islamic cult as we find another meteorite that somehow holds some portion of the ancient Arabian goddess of fate and destiny, and the personification of the evening star or Manat [one of the daughters of the pre-Islamic Allah]. This is sort of a cult within a cult which is present between Medina and Mecca, where Manat was worshipped in the form of another black meteorite stone representing a different form of the moon god or possibly even a different god all together.

Archeologists Must Stay Quiet

Because the "religion" hinges on Arabia's pre-Islamic history, its god/goddess basics seem to be kept as a closely guarded secret. For instance, it has been reported that archaeologists working in Saudi Arabia are sworn to secrecy. However, multiple artifacts have been found, which show that the Moon and the Star symbol of Islam was pre-Islamic and associated with Moon Worship.

No Other Gods

Can you just see one of the Islamic "followers" kissing one of those meteorites and saying there is no God except Allah and Mohammed is his messenger----except the gods associated with this rock--- oh yes there are Jinns as well---

We'll get into the subject of Jinns later, but they arte simply people who are invisible. One more thing about these people is that they are made out of fire, so they are slightly different than "Normal" people.

Crescent Moon Symbol

The identical Ishtar crescent moon thing began showing up everywhere a mosque or Islamic representation was undertaken. This almost sounds like the Islamic God is a Crescent Moon God. Here are a few of the Crescent moon symbols to consider here.

- "Allah" was also the personal name given to the moon god, the highest of <u>the 360 pagan idols</u> worshipped in Mecca, Muhammad's home town. He would have prayed to them even at a very young age.
- Consider what the pagan Arabians did to worship their moon god, Allah; they prayed while bowing towards Kabah, the "house of Allah".
- In Mecca that houses a meteorite - a stone from space - several times a day, visited it once a year, and walked around it several times during their visit.
- The Muslim "holy" month of Ramadan starts at the sighting of a new crescent moon.
- Perched atop churches across the world is the cross, the symbol of the sacrifice made by our God. Perched atop

mosques across the world is the crescent moon, the symbol of Allah whom Muhammad chose as the God of Islam.

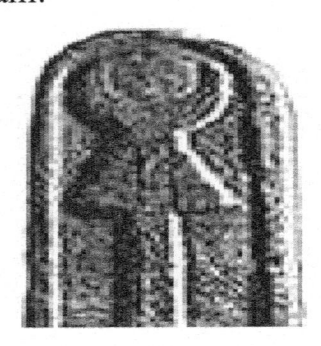

- To this day, Allah's "Moon god" origins are visible on the tops of countless mosques, for example on the tops of the twin towers of the Great Mosque in Mecca, where you can see the "crescent Moon" symbol, which represented the "Moon god" in the Ancient Middle East.
- The crescent Moon symbol is also on the top of the Maqam Ibrahim structure beside Mecca's Kaba shrine, which is the holiest place in the world for Muslims.
- Finally, the same symbol is on the flags of some mostly-Muslim nations (Algeria, Azerbaijan, Malaysia, the Maldives, Mauritania, Pakistan, Turkey, and Uzbekistan), on the flag which Libya's National Transitional Council have adopted, and on the sides of the ambulances which the Muslim equivalent of the Red Cross (the Red Crescent) operate, though those flags, and the Red Crescent emblem, were thought up long after Muslims began putting symbols of Allah the Moon god on the tops of their early mosques, and are thus, unlike those mosques, not proof of Allah's Moon god origins.
- The Kaba shrine contains a famous black meteorite, which landed at the site of what became Mecca. Pre-

Muslim Arabians revered the space rock, as they did not know what meteorites were, which led them to believe that their Supreme Deity had sent them the rock. So, they built the Kaba shrine to Allah at the meteorite's impact site. Mecca then developed around the Moon god's shrine, because the desert Bedouins made pilgrimages to the place, where they thought Allah had sent them a space rock.

- The fact that Muslims regard what was primarily a shrine to a pre-Muslim lunar deity as their holiest place is, of course, further proof that Allah was originally a "Moon god". Why did Mohammed not build a new shrine for the God of his new religion instead of simply taking over one, which was already devoted to Allah the "Moon god"?

- The fact that, to this day, when Muslims make their pilgrimage to Mecca, they kiss or touch the black meteorite in the Kaba. This is more proof that Allah was originally a lunar deity. Why did Mohammed not create a new "holy relic" for Muslims to kiss or touch, instead of telling them to kiss or touch Allah the Moon god's "holy relic"?

- Although the word "Allah" simply means "the God", the fact that Muhammad did not invent a new name for his new Muslim god when he invented Islam is, of course, even more proof that Allah' was originally a "lunar deity".

- There is no debate about the fact that the Moon God worshipping Meccans referred to their supreme deity as Allah' before Mohammed. This is why a man called Abd-Allah – meaning "servant of Allah", or "slave of Allah" – lived in Mecca before Muhammad and that man was very <u>Muhammad's father</u>. His Banu Hashim clansmen of the

Quraysh tribe were pious devotees of their Moon god, as they were in charge of looking after the Kaba shrine.

- Abd-Allah was not given a new Muslim name after Muhammad invented Islam, because Abd-Allah died 6 months before Muhammad was born. Moreover, even Muhammad had given one of his sons the name Abd-Allah well before he began inventing Islam at the age of 40 by writing the "Quran".

War More Important Than Sex?

Sex is hugely important to the Islamic cultist. He dreams about how his killing will allow him to attain heaven so that he will have an endless supply of virgin sex objects. The reason there is so much sex is not that the Moon God wants it, Mohammed showed his followers the way to live as the perfect follower of the Moon God and he liked sex; a lot of sex.

The Quran doesn't have as much sex in it as the other holy books, but they make up for what is missing in the Quran, which is the smallest of the three books, the Trilogy. It is only 14% of the Trilogy text. This means that the Sunna [Description of Mohammed being perfect] is 86% of the word content of Islam's sacred texts. This statistic alone has large implications. Most of the Islamic doctrine is about Mohammed, not Allah. The Quran says 91 different times that Mohammed is the perfect pattern of life. It is much more important to know Mohammed than the Quran. What Mohammed liked as much as sex was war and killing. It turns out that jihad occurs in large proportion in all three texts as well. Here is a chart about the results:

Amount of Text Devoted to Jihad

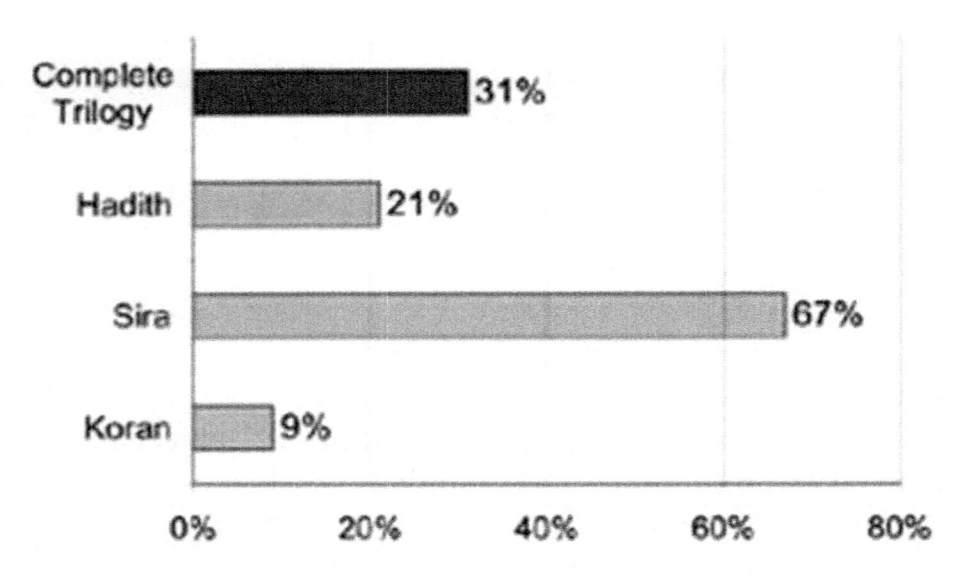

Source	Percentage
Complete Trilogy	31%
Hadith	21%
Sira	67%
Koran	9%

It is very significant that the Sira devotes 67% of its text to jihad and here is another statistic. Mohammed averaged an event of violence every 6 weeks for the last 9 years of his life. Jihad was what made Mohammed successful and it is what Islam is based on OK! It is based on SEX and Jihad, but you know what I mean. There is no love as continuously described in Christian teachings.

Mohammed is Sunna

All Muslims agree that: "There is no god, but Allah and Mohammed is His messenger."

When this is repeated as a public testimony, you become a Muslim. However, this statement is not only the beginning of Islam; it is also the foundation and totality of Islam. It is not enough to worship Allah; you must worship as Mohammed worshipped.

<u>Who is Allah and where do we learn about Him? This question points directly to the Quran.</u>

Then the Quran, in turn, points directly to Mohammed. It says 91 times that Mohammed is the perfect Muslim. He is the divine human prototype, the only pattern acceptable to Allah.

<u>The actions and words of Mohammed are so important that they have a special name—Sunna. We find the Sunna in two texts, Hadith and Sira</u>.

The Sira is the biography of Mohammed and the Hadith is the collection of hadiths (small stories, traditions) about Mohammed.

<u>This is because Mohammed is the ultimate example [SUNNA] of how Allah wants everyone to live.</u>

Islam is based on Quran and Sunna. Since the Sunna is found in the Sira and the Hadith, this means that three books contain **all the doctrine of Islam**—the Trilogy. If it is in the Trilogy (Quran, Sira, Hadith), then it is Islam. If something is not in the Trilogy, then it is not Islam. All of the Islamic doctrine is found in the Trilogy. Now, we have the complete information with no missing pieces.

We have established our first criteria of knowledge. All authoritative statements about Islam must include a reference to the Trilogy to be authenticated. It does not matter what a scholar, imam, media guru, or anyone else says, if what they say cannot be supported by the doctrine in the Trilogy, then it is not Islam. If it is supported by the Trilogy, then it is Islam.

Quran Not the Main Book

We have been taught that the Quran is the source of Islamic doctrine but the Sunna texts make up 86% so Islam is 14% Allah and 86% Mohammed...

Mohammed is the perfect example of how to live the sacred life for the Moon God. This idea of complete, final, universal, and perfect textual truth is very hard for non-Muslims to comprehend. Most people read the Quran with the attitude that they don't really believe this. Unfortunately, when Muslims read the Quran, their attitude is: "These are the perfect words of Allah." Muslims call themselves the "believers" and by that they mean that they believe the Quran is perfect and Mohammed is the perfect pattern of life.

The Quran of the bookstore is not the historical Quran of Mohammed, because Uthman, a caliph (supreme ruler) had it arranged starting with the longest chapter and ending at the shortest chapter. After he created the Quran we know today, he burned the originals. The time and story have been annihilated by the rearrangement. From a statistical point of view, the text was randomized and, hence, very difficult to understand.

Misconception About Christianity

It has been said that more people have died in the name of Christianity than any other religion. This is simply is not the truth. While there have been some aberrations in Christianity that have been simply awful, since the advent of true Christian beliefs that have been organized in any reasonable fashion there has been very few.

Christians were thrown to the lions and used as human torches during the Roman times. Emperor Constantine decided that making Christianity a State religion would make him popular so The Council of Nicaea built an organized religion and a "canonized" text in 325AD. 1800 Bishops took part in determination of what **"The State Religion"** would agree to do. The problem is that while this powerful State Religion was created, it was not built around ideals of the Bible. A Pope was put in place that would be the-

"Intercessor between God and people"

-and no one was allowed to interpret Biblical texts besides their bishops, monks and learned priests "skilled" in the INTERPRETATION of the Hebrew and Latin words.

What a mess.

Soon, their power was pushed throughout the land. Popes got more powerful that Kings when the State Religion mantra was to NOT USURP power, but have a passive communal religion. Don't get this group confused with today's Catholic Religion. Today's Catholic Church is significantly different, this ancient monstrosity was a farce as tiny groups of Christians met to learn and understand what the Biblical teachings were had to hid for their Christian beliefs. It got so bad, the term CHURCH was substituted for the made-up word CONGREGATION so that no one would think they were talking about the massive State Religion Church. They completely ignored the Holy books of Christianity, sold favors, and had complete control of people lives and liberties. They insured the people would not read and understand the Biblical teaching so that they could hold on to power. It was this thing that initiated the bloody Crusades, exterminations of Jews, Moslems, and Christians alike. Here are some highlights. To be fair, The Moslems had forced their way into the "Holy Land with a substantial amount of killing well before the Crusades so there was some reasonable action being done, but the State Religion went too far.

408-"State Religion" and Emperor Theodosius (408-450) - This guy even had **children executed**, because they had been playing with remains of pagan statues.

372-444 AD "Christians against the State Religion" Called Manichaean heresy: a Christian group was slaughtered for practicing birth control all over the Roman Empire. Many thousands of victims were killed.

782-Emperor Karl (Charlemagne) had over 4 thousand Pagan Saxons, unwilling to convert to State Christianity, beheaded. I know this sounds Islamic, but this was the result of the hugely powerful State Religion against Jew, Christian, Moslem and Pagan alike.

1095 First "State Religion" Crusade: on command of Pope Urban II, thousands of Jews and Moslems were slain in Semlin/Hungary; thousands more in Wieselburg/Hungary. In Nikaia, Xerigordon there were thousands more. By 1098, a total of 40 capital cities and 200 castles were conquered and death was everywhere.

1098-99 Second State Religion Crusade: Antiochia and Marra were conquered and many thousands were killed. Because of the subsequent famine "the already stinking corpses of the enemies were eaten by the State Religion Believers" according to historian Albert Aquensis. By **1099, Jerusalem** was conquered and multiple thousands of Moslems and Jews were piled on the streets.

1204 Fourth "State Religion" Crusade: Constantinople was sacked, number of Moslem victims numbered in the **thousands;** many of theses were on the State Religion side.

1291- Other Crusades- until the fall of Akkon 1291 well over a million victims were counted as loss during this bloody time.

1209 "Christians against State Religion" This was the first "Crusade" intended to slay Christians. The Albigensians were Christians that would not accept State rule, and taxes, and prohibition of birth control. Under Pope Innocent III (sometimes called the greatest single pre-Nazi mass murderer) destroyed, <u>**all**</u> the inhabitants of Bezir, France [many thousand]. In Carcassonne thousands more were slain. Other cities followed. After 20 years of war, nearly all

Cathars (probably half of southern France) were exterminated. Luckily, Innocent III died in 1217.

1229 Crusades were over and hometown Inquisitions could commence. It has been estimated that hundreds of thousands of Christian Cathar victims were killed in very brutal ways for stating that what the New Testament called the Prince of the Earth could be considered an evil God. Other heresies of the State Religion included the Waldensians, Paulikians, Runcarians, Josephites, and many others. Most of these sects were exterminated; at least hundred thousand victims.

1234-Peasants of Steding Germany were unwilling to pay suffocating "State Religion" taxes just like the Moslems required for their conquered enemies. Thousands of men, women and children were slain by the huge State Religion zealots.

1337-1350- German State Religion Zealots- Starting in Deggendorf/Germany a Jew-killing craze reaches 51 towns in Bavaria, Austria, Poland. By 1349, in more than 350 towns in Germany all Jews murdered, many burned alive. In this one year, more Jews were killed than Christians in the 200 years of ancient Roman persecution of Christians.

1389-1391 In Prag 3,000 Jews were slaughtered. 1391 Seville's Jews were killed with Archbishop Martinez leading the slaughter of 4,000 with 25,000 sold as slaves.

1456-Battle of Belgrad- During this episode, there may have been up to 80,000 Moslems slaughtered.

15th century Poland- Thousands of Christian and Jewish villages were plundered by State Religion Knights of the Order. Thousands were killed.

16th and 17th century Ireland- English troops "pacified and civilized" Ireland. **Tens of thousands** of Pagan Gaelic Irish fell victim to the State Religion.

I know this doesn't sound like Christianity identified in the New Testament Writings. It was not in any way Christian. It almost sounds like the people were fighting for egomaniacal rulers similar to the horrors of Nazi Germany. Here is the difference between the Islamic "faith" and this "State Church" rampage. The State Church Holy Books in no way sanctioned, desired, declared, or required this type of action, but the Nazi and Islamic books of action absolutely come from their holy books. Some might say the Nazi instructions were not holy and many would say the Islamic "books" cannot be holy either. During the whole Crusade period, people were chanted "Hip-hip-hurray", but some have forgotten what it means.

Hip Hip Hurray

If you ever wondered why someone would say such a thing, it comes for those crusaders. The word HIP comes from the initials of "Hieroso Iyma est Pedita" [Jerusalem has fallen]. The "hurray" part is actually older and come from the Slavic language for "To Paradise". Therefore, you and I are really saying "Jerusalem has fallen, on to paradise." What a thing to say at a ball game!

Inquisition

As I mentioned, it wasn't long before the STATE CHURCH needed a new outlet as the Crusades became sadder and sadder ending with the Children's Crusade. I knew it was a shock to find that most of the children didn't make it home. The "church" continued to drive out Pagans, Moslems, Jews, and Christian "Heretics" of the State Religion from just about all the civilized areas of Europe. The way this was done varied, but it always meant killing. Joan of Arc ---killed for wearing pants. Those accused of not doing what the State Religion required---killed. Many times, they were killed by burning at the stake or some horrible way to die similar to those proposed by the modern Islamic Cult of today. There is no wonder, Christians are labeled as monsters. This horrible time was not Christian; it was not sanctioned by Christianity. It was not identified, written about, or allowed in ANY New Testament teaching---- it was not Christian it was just murder just like the TEACHINGS of Mohammed address murder and it was accomplished by a State controlled religion just like the Islamic State run religion.

William Tyndale and Martin Luther

In the 1500's things changed. While splinter Christian groups tried there best to worship, the might CHURCH destroyed many. Then, 2 men Martin Luther and William Tyndale decided the only way for Christianity to survive would be for people to be able to read the Bible. If they read the Bible, they would know the horrors of the State Religion, so they made English and German Bibles and everything changed. Certainly, Tyndale died as his body was engulfed in English Flames and Luther continued to evade the most aggressive action by the State Church to extinguish Christianity, but Bibles were made. Christianity that had taken shape in hidden places during this horrible time now came out in the open. A brand new Catholicism took control of the remaining elements of the State Church to reassert Christian beliefs. Since that time, the Aggressive killing has been mostly associated with something well removed from Christianity.

What's the Difference?

Some will try to convince you that the blood thirsty Christians were the brutal killers simply because the State Church claimed to be Christian, but there is no truth in it. There is no call for war in Christian Literature. There is no call for killing, call for Jihad, or call for worship of a demented sex crazed, power hungry, and cult leader. The Islamic religion is FILLED with these things to get to a paradise filled with debauchery. Please don't think they are in any way similar and that Christianity has been the source of all the killing before the 1500s. It just is not so!!!!!!

OK! Christianity must take some of the blame, but let's look at what is missing from this Islamic cult by just reading a small segment of the New Testament of the Christian Bible.

Christian God Preached Love of ALL

Mohammed the Anti-Christ

Throughout the entire New Testament used as the cornerstone of Christianity, the word love continues. Love God, Love, your Enemies, and Love you masters. The message is love everyone. That is what Christianity preaches. Here is just a small segment from the book of I John. **First we find that anyone <u>not</u> preaching words of LOVE are from the ANTICHRIST.** It is saying Mohammed, along with others doing similar horrible things were anti-christs.

*1 John 4:1-4- Dear friends, do not believe every spirit, but test the spirits to see whether they are from God, because many false prophets have gone out into the world. This is how you can recognize the Spirit of God: Every spirit that acknowledges that Jesus Christ has come in the flesh is from God, but **<u>every spirit that does not acknowledge Jesus is not from God. This is the spirit of the antichrist</u>**, which you have heard is coming and even now is already in the world.*

Teachings of Love

1 John 4:7-21- Dear friends, let us <u>love one another</u>, for <u>love comes from God. Everyone who loves has been born of God</u> and knows God. Whoever does not love does not know God, because <u>God is love</u>. This is how <u>God showed his love</u> among us: He sent his one and only Son into the world that we might live through him. <u>This is love</u>: not that <u>we loved</u>

God, but that *he loved us* and sent his Son as an atoning sacrifice for our sins. Dear friends, since *God so loved* us, we also ought to *love one another*. No one has ever seen God; but if we *love one another*, God lives in us and *his love is made complete* in us. This is how we know that we live in him and he in us: He has given us of his Spirit. And we have seen and testify that the Father has sent his Son to be the Savior of the world. If anyone acknowledges that Jesus is the Son of God, God lives in them and they in God. And so we know and rely on *the love God has for us*. *God is love*. Whoever lives in *love lives in God*, and God in them. This is how *love is made complete* among us so that we will have confidence on the Day of Judgment: In this world, we are like Jesus. There is *no fear in love*. But *perfect love drives out fear*, because fear has to do with punishment. The one who fears is not made *perfect in love*. *We love* because *he first loved us*. Whoever claims to *love God* yet hates a brother or sister is a liar. For *whoever does not love* their brother and sister, whom they have seen, *cannot love God*, whom they have not seen. And he has given us this command: *Anyone who loves God* must *love their brother and sister*.

It's almost like poetry. The Moon God Prophet, on the other hand, changes all the love to hate and says Kill pagans, kill Christians, kill Jews, and even kill yourself. Hate everyone that is not Moslem, and do everything in your power to take control of the entire world. To do this you must lie, cheat, steal, and kill your way to a sex heaven. With that let's look at Islamic Law.

Islamic Law

If have read the 10 commandments and the 612 Jewish Laws of isolation which tried earnestly to insure the Jewish Nation would not marry or have relations outside their group, you probably were somewhat confused until you realized the idea behind the laws was to completely separate the Jews from the rest of the world. Well, the Arab Islamics decided that they should follow the Adamic Isolation Laws for some reason, but they believed that the Jewish laws were all misinterpreted. They modified them to be more in line with what they wanted them to say. According to "the Quran 6:151-153", they limited the sex laws but made the rest of them twisted so that they could get around them.

1. **Don't worship other gods** besides the moon God Allah'. [This included Yahweh, by the way.]
2. Be good to your parents, but **kill your children** on a plea of want. [Don't be shocked as this is a very minor killing requirement. It turned into honor killing which will be discussed later.]
3. Don't be lewd, even in secret. [This is a strange one in that lewdness was completely ignored when it came to servants. Islamics simply say they are owned by my right hand so there is no such thing as lewdness.]
4. Don't kill, except for justice or the law. [In this case the law gives great authority to kill a lot, so don't feel they

were restricted. After all, Mohammed was writing the law and liked killing.]

5. **Do not have sex** with your mothers, your daughters, your sisters, and the sisters of your fathers, the sisters of your mothers, the daughters of your brother, and the daughters of your sister. [These certainly make sense, but they didn't stop there and they have now changed the law to allow boys to have sex with their sisters so that they can concentrate on Jihad better.] I know Moslems are supposed to have 4 wives and many sex slaves, but this is the beginning of their law right now.

6. Do not marry two sisters at the same time or have sex with the women who were married to your genetic sons, the mothers of your wives, or the daughters of your wives with whom you have consummated the marriage. [Although no genetic problems would occur, the Islamic extended the "No sex list" beyond the Jewish laws, possibly showing that these were significant problems during the time when Mohammed wrote them.] [He even gave himself a special dispensation to allow him to take his son-in law's wife as his 5th wife.]

7. Don't have sex with your nursing mothers, or the girls who nursed from the same woman as you. [Somehow, their god supposedly thought that milk would cause problems. As mentioned before, this law has also been rescinded to allow for a better jihad.]

Later I will expand on this very small set to show how dangerous these people can truly be. One way is to assert history AFTER the fact. I know it sounds like Jews and Moslems were almost bickering over the same things. Some of the bickering focuses on the Dome of the Rock.

Dome of the Rock Fake Ascension

"Thou Shalt Hate Jews" [called monkeys or Apes in the Koran]. That's one of the laws of Islam. I know you're thinking the hatred goes back to the time of Ishmael and Isaac, but let me tell you that when their father died, we are told both sons buried their father and worshipped together, so there was not a running feud or uncontrollable hatred, but you would have to say part of this hatred is fostered by Jews living in a holy area that Moslems believe was meant for them. Miraculously, Jerusalem was supposed to be the ascension place for Mohammed and the place where a magical meteorite was placed. The problem is that the ascension place, called the Dome of the Rock, could not possibly have been in Jerusalem. Here are a few items to consider.

Mohammed would not have gone to a Christian church for his ascension. In or around 711, or about 80 years after Mohammed died, Abd El-Wahd, who ruled from 705-715, reconstructed the Christian-Byzantine Church of St. Mary and converted it into a mosque. All he added was an onion-like dome on top of the building and the Crescent Moon image for the moon god to make it look like a mosque. He then named it El-Aksa, which sounds similar to the Ascension location identified in the Quran. *[El-Mi'araj means Ascending Place]*

Mohammed could never have had this mosque in mind when he compiled the Quran, since it did not exist for another three generations after his death.

Mohammed issued a strict prohibition against facing Jerusalem in prayer, on February 12, 624. Jerusalem simply never held any sanctity for the Moslems according to Mohammed himself. Now it is a requirement.

The mosque in question was not considered sacred for another thousand years after it was built, in fact, the picture below shows the dilapidated condition of this "unholy" landmark in 1875. Note the heavy grass intrusion, the disrepair of the roof. Note, also, how many worshippers are in and around the place.

If the Moslems would consider the possibility that the place of Ascension was another location, there might not be as much unrest between the two nations and if the Jews realized that God giving them the land flowing with milk and honey didn't mean land on earth, their side might also give some leeway. In this case, it seems that misinterpreted history did more than just keep people ignorant. It made them and is still making them kill each other.

The Moslems just made up the Dome of the Rock thing so that they would have a Good Reason for Hating.

One thing to hate as a Moslem is Satan. Here are a few things to note before we get into more detailed analysis.

Moslem Satan

Here are some of the Moslem works concerning Satan. This comes from "Hadith of Bukhari" volume 4, one of the 3 most holy books in the religion. This work is second only to the Quran in importance and authority, are collections of Islamic traditions and laws (25 thousand of them). This includes traditional sayings of Muhammad and later Islamic sages. As you read these, understand that they are 100 percent true according to all that makes us Islam.

516: Satan in the Nose-The Prophet said, "If anyone of you rouses from sleep and performs the ablution, he should wash his nose by putting water in it and then blowing it out thrice, because **Satan has stayed in the upper part of his nose** all the night."

509:The Satan Yawn-The Prophet said, "<u>Yawning is from Satan</u> and if anyone of you yawns, he should check his yawning as much as possible, for if anyone of you (during the act of yawning) should say: **'Ha', Satan will laugh at him."**

The Quran also talks about Satan, but not quite as colorfully. This is saying number 117. *The Pagans, leaving Him [Allah], Call but upon female deities: They call but upon Satan, the persistent rebel!* This is strange in that the Moon

Diminish Women

God originally was female. Mohammed changed its sex early on to diminish the power of women. Another way to diminish the power of women is to kill them.

Murder the Neda

Neda are people who try to advance the cause of freedom in the Islamic world by not renouncing their religion, holding inappropriate books, or speaking out against the Islamic cult.

You're not going to like this, but, murder, and rape are part of this discussion. The first Nedas are described below.

Since the revolution in Iran, two thousand women have been hanged as Neda. They don't hang like we think of it. Rather than using a hangman's noose to snap the neck quickly, these victims were slowly pulled into the air kicking and flailing until they finally suffocated. The girl above, Mona, was the first of this long list of martyrs for freedom. She was only 17.

Another, Taraneh, was a veterinary student who died with her mother. If you are thinking this is a nice CULT Religion please understand that 187 of the first Nedas slowly and painfully executed were under the age of 18, with 9 girls under the age of 13. The youngest girl executed was just 10 years old, but they had a problem. Under the law, young girls who were sentenced to death could not be executed if they were still virgins, so they had to be raped first and married to one of the guards. After the execution, a marriage certificate was sent to the victim's family along with a box of sweets to show true hatred for females and the families that did not control these young girls and women.

Kafir

Moslems aren't just horrible to women; there are the Kafirs which include just about everyone that is not a Moslem. Islam devotes a great amount of energy to the Kafir. Not only is the majority (64%) of the Quran devoted to the Kafir, but also nearly all of the Sira (81%) deals with Mohammed's struggle with them. The Hadith (Traditions of Mohammed) devotes 32% of the text to Kafirs. 60% of the entire Trilogy text is devoted to the Kafir, but the details are muttled.

They initially sound just like Normal religion with tolerance to the Kafir.

Quran 2:219 says that Muslims should be tolerant and forgiving to People of the Book [Bible using Kafir].

<u>As you read farther, the truth comes out in ALL cases.</u>

Quran 9:29 says to attack the People of the Book [Bible using Kafir] until they pay the jizyah, the dhimmi tax, submit to Sharia law and be humbled.

Quran 5.60- God has cursed the Jews, transforming them into apes and swine and those who serve the devil.

Quran 9.29- Fight against such of those have been given the Scriptures, Jews and Christians, as believe not in Allah nor the last Day

As we read further, the language gets worse and worse. Which Quran shows the true nature of Islam?

Everyone knows of good verses in the Quran. In fact, 245 verses in the Quran say something positive about Kafirs. However, **in every case**, the Quran is followed by another Quran that contradicts the "good" verses.

Here is the rule of thumb.

The farther back in the three holy books you read the more relevant and important. Essentially all of the nice little sayings are fluff to hide the truth.

Don't just hear what they want you to hear---Start at the back. One thing you will notice is there is a lot of killing required. Even the Kafirs are to be murdered.

Hate Jews Sunna

Here are a sample of Allah's teachings and commands regarding the Jews and how to become more perfect. A Jew is sort of a special Kafir.

Quran 2.61 *Wretchedness and baseness were stamped on the Jews and they were visited with wrath from Allah.*

Quran 2:96 *Jews are the greediest of all humankind. They'd like to live 1000 years. But <u>they are going to hell</u>.*

***Quran 4:160*-*1** *For the wrongdoing Jews, Allah has prepared a painful doom.*

Quran 4.16 *And for the evildoing of the Jews, we have forbidden them from some good things that were previously permitted them.*

Quran 5.82 *Indeed you will surely find that <u>the most vehement of men</u> in enmity to those who believe are the Jews and the polytheists.*

Quran 5.60 *<u>God has cursed the Jews</u>, transforming them into <u>apes and swine</u> and those who serve the devil.*

Quran 9.29 *Fight against such of those have been given the Scriptures, <u>Jews and Christians</u>, as believe not in Allah nor the last Day.*

Quran 9.34 *Many of the <u>Jewish rabbis and the monks devour the wealth of mankind</u> and wantonly debar men from the way of Allah.*

Quran 62.5 *A hypocritical <u>Jew looks like an ass carrying books.</u> Those who deny the revelations of Allah are ugly.*

Bukhari 19:4366*: the Messenger of Allah said: "<u>I will expel the Jews and Christians from the Arabian Peninsula</u> and will not leave any but Muslim."*

Bukhari 4:52:288*-The Prophet on his death-bed, gave three orders one of them was to <u>Expel the pagans</u> from the Arabian Peninsula.*

Quran-33:27*- "And He made you heirs of their lands [confiscated all the Jewish land], their houses, and their goods, and of a land which ye had not frequented before. And Allah has power over all things."*

Murder All Kafirs

Kafir means anyone not an Islamic, so these guys are ordered to kill everyone. The Jews, Hindu, and Christians seemed to be the worst of the Kafirs, but they are pretty much open to anyone.

Murder the Pagans

Quran 9:5: *"Then, when the sacred months have passed, slay the idolaters [Hindu] wherever ye find them, and take them (captive), and besiege them, and prepare for them each ambush. But if they repent and establish worship and pay the poor-due [become Muslim], then leave their way free. Lo! Allah is Forgiving, Merciful."* HA!!!

Quran 22:19-22: *"for them (the unbelievers) <u>garments of fire shall be cut and there shall be poured over their heads boiling water</u> whereby whatever is in their bowels and <u>skin shall be dissolved</u> and they will be <u>punished with hooked iron rods</u>."*

Does boiling water over a head, dissolving someone's skin and insides, or a hooked iron rod punishments sound sane??? This is the will of the MOON GOD!!!

Murder Christians and Jews

Quran 9:29: *"<u>Fight against such of those **who have been given the Scripture** [especially the Holy Bible] as believe not in Allah</u> nor the Last Day, and forbid not that which Allah hath forbidden by His messenger, and follow not the Religion of Truth, until they pay the tribute readily, being brought low."*

Quran 5:72- *Christians will burn in the fire.*

Notice something very important here. It says that if you believe in the God of the Bible, you do not believe in the Allah of Islam.

This verse sanctifies the attacking and killing of Jews and Christians, until they are defeated and submitted to the supremacy of Islam and in willing humiliation, pay submission tax to Muslims. **Below is a simple killing of a Christian by fire by MODERATE Muslims desiring to fulfil requirements of the Moon God.**

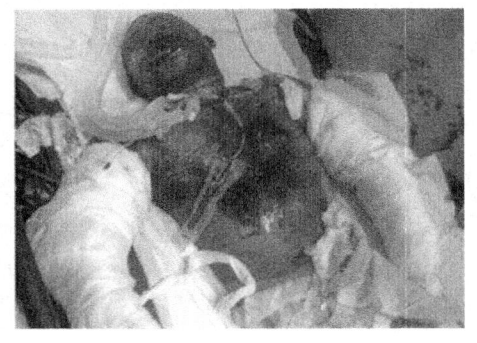

QURAN 5:72 Christians will burn in the fire.

Christian Rape and Torture

The next images are of a small Christian girl raped, tortured and murdered as per Quran.

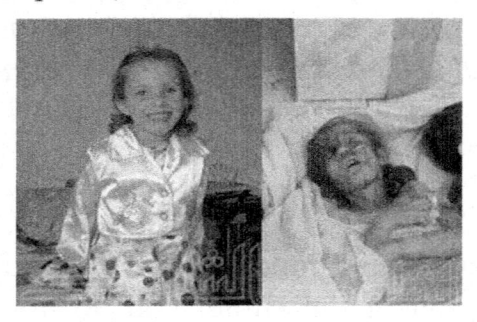

Quran 4:24, *"And all married women are forbidden unto you save those captives whom your right hand possess."*

Sold as a slave, this one never came out of slavery, but paid the price for not being a good sex partner.

Murder Jews

Quran-33:25- *"Allah turned back the unbelievers [Meccans and their allies the Jewish Banu Qurayza] in a state of rage, having not won any good, and Allah spared the believers battle. Allah is, indeed, Strong and Mighty." [There was a slaughter of the Banu Qurayza.]*

Quran-33:26- *"And He brought those of the People of the Book [Jewish people of Banu Qurayza] who supported them from their fortresses and cast terror into their hearts, some of them you slew (beheaded) and some you took prisoners (captive)"*

Bukhari 4:52:176- *Allah's Apostle said, "You Muslims will fight with the Jews till some of them will hide behind stones. The stones will betray them saying, slave of Allah! There is a Jew hiding behind me; so kill him.' "*

Rasul 553 *"the Apostle of Allah said, 'Kill any Jew that falls into your power."]*

Bukhari 4:52:176-177: *"Allah's Apostle said, 'The Hour will not be established until you fight with the Jews, and the stone behind which a Jew will be hiding will say. " O Muslim! There is a Jew hiding behind me, so kill him."'*

It's bad when stones are forced by the moon God to speak, but there you have it. Poor Jews have no chance if even the stones hate them. Speaking of hate, the Moslems even hate the Hindu that are pretty much passive.

There are 22 Categories of Islamic Murder with 52 Reasons Muslim Men Can Kill Sanctioned by Allah. You come up with an irritation, and you can probably find out that Islamics fix issues with murder. In a way, it is a simple religion.

His inhuman teachings have inspired the slaughter of an estimated 270,000,000 kafirs, over the last 1400 years, by Muslims in their aim to fulfill the teaching of Quran 9:111 for gaining a place in his whorehouse Paradise.

Hell for Christians and Jews

Quran 4:55 *"Sufficient for them is Hell and the Flaming Fire! Those [Jews] who disbelieve Our Revelations shall be cast into Hell. When their skin is burnt up and singed, we shall give them a new coat that they may go on tasting the agony of punishment."*

Quran 73:11 *"Leave Me alone to deal **with the believers** (those who believe in "the book"). Respite those who possess good things for a little while. Verily, with us are heavy shackles (to bind), a raging fire (to burn them), food that chokes, and a torturous penalty of painful doom."*

Quran 74:31 *"We have appointed nineteen angels to be the wardens of the Hell Fire. We made a stumbling-block for those who disbelieve and We have fixed their number as a trial for unbelievers in order that the People of the Book [Christians and Jews] may arrive with certainty, and that no doubts may be left for the people of the Book, those in whose hearts is a disease."*

Murder For Leaving Islam

Not only are they to kill all the Kafirs but their own people are supposed to be killed.

Quran 5:33: Allah said about apostates "*they shall be killed or crucified or their hands and feet be cut off from the opposite sides, or exiled from the land. That is their disgrace in this world; and a great torment is theirs in the hereafter.*"

Quran 4:89: "*They but wish that ye should reject Faith, as they do, and thus be on the same footing (as they): But take not friends from their ranks until they flee in the way of Allah. But if they turn renegades, seize them and **slay them** wherever ye find them; and take no friends or helpers from their ranks;*"

Ishaq: 550: "*The reason that Allah's Messenger ordered Abdullash Bin Sarh slain was because he had become a Muslim and used to write down Quran Revelation. Then he rejected Islam after becoming suspicious of some verses which prophet changed after his suggestions.*"

Ishaq: 551: "*The Messenger ordered Miqyas' assassination, because he became a renegade by rejecting Islam.*"

Bukhari, 4:52:260: "*The Prophet said, 'If a Muslim discards his religion, kill him.*"

Bukhari 5:59:632: "*Once Muadh paid a visit to Abu Musa and saw a chained man. Muadh asked, "What is this?" Abu

Musa said, "(He was) a Jew who embraced Islam and has now **rejected Islam**." Muadh said, "I will surely chop off his neck!"

Bukhari 52:260 - "...The Prophet said, 'If somebody (a Muslim) discards his religion, **kill him**.'"

Bukhari 83:37 - "Allah's Apostle never killed anyone except in one of the following three situations: (1) A person who killed somebody unjustly, was killed (in Qisas,) (2) a married person who committed illegal sexual intercourse and (3) a man who fought against Allah and His Apostle and **deserted Islam and became an apostate**."

Bukhari 84:57 - "[In the words of] Allah's Apostle, 'Whoever changed his Islamic religion, then **kill him**.'"

Bukhari 89:271 - A man who embraces Islam, then reverts to Judaism **is to be killed** according to "the verdict of Allah and his apostle."

Bukhari 84:5 - "There was a fettered man beside Abu Muisa. Mu'adh asked, 'who is this (man)?' Abu Muisa said, 'He was a Jew and became a Muslim and then reverted back to Judaism.' Then Abu Muisa requested Mu'adh to sit down but Mu'adh said, 'I will not sit down **till he has been killed**. This is the judgment of Allah and His Apostle (for such cases) and repeated it thrice.' Then Abu Musa ordered that the man **be killed,** and he **was killed**. Abu Musa added, "Then we discussed the night prayers."

Bukhari (84:64-65 - "Allah's Apostle: 'During the last days there will appear some young foolish people who will say the best words but their faith will not go beyond their throats (they will have no faith) and will go out from their religion as an arrow goes out of the game. So, wherever you find them, **kill them**, for **whoever kills them shall have reward** on the Day of Resurrection.'

Murder For Not Converting

Here, "corruption in the land" means rejecting Islam and continue practicing other religions. And extermination of such people is commanded in this verse. The apostates of Islam, by rejecting Islam, create corruption in the land; Muslim women, who demand equality with men, rejecting what Allah has ordained, create corruption in the land; Muslim girls in the West, who reject Islamic way of life and adopt the Western culture, create corruption in the land; and so on.

Quran 5:32: *"For that cause We decreed for the Children of Israel that whosoever killeth a human being for other than manslaughter or <u>corruption in the earth</u>, it shall be as if he had killed all mankind, and whoso saveth the life of one, it shall be as if he had saved the life of all mankind. Our messengers came unto them of old with clear proofs (of Allah's Sovereignty), but afterwards lo! Many of them became prodigals in the earth."*

It should be noted that while this Quran gives license to summary murder of innocent people, <u>President Obama quoted the above passage in his Cairo speech as a symbol of sublime humanity of Islam. Here is another passage.</u>

Quran 5:33*: "The only reward of those who make war upon Allah and His messenger and strive after corruption [not converting] in the land will be that <u>they will be killed or crucified</u>, or have their hands and feet on alternate sides cut off, or **<u>will be expelled</u>** out of the land. Such will be their degradation in the world, and in the Hereafter theirs will be an awful doom;"*

Quran 47:4*:"Therefore, when ye meet the **<u>Kafirs (Unbelievers in fight), smite at their necks;</u>** At length, when ye have thoroughly subdued them, bind a bond firmly: thereafter (is the time for) either generosity or ransom: Until the war lays down its burdens. Thus (are ye commanded): but if it had been Allah's Will, He could certainly have exacted retribution from them (Himself); but (He lets you fight) in order to test you, some with others. But **<u>those who are slain in the Way of Allah</u>**, - He will never let their deeds be lost."*

Self Murder and Terrorism

If you want to get frightened of these guys, read the next few verses of anti-love, terrorism, and Martyrdom. I want you to remember that these words are in THEIR BIBLE!!!!

Quran 4:74: *"Let those fight in the cause of God Who sell the life of this world for the hereafter. To him who fighteth in the cause of God, - whether **he is slain or gets victory - Soon shall we give him a reward** of great (value)?"*

Quran 2:207: *"And there is the type of man **who gives his life to earn the pleasure of God**: And God is full of kindness to (His) devotees."*

Quran 8:60 *"Against them make ready your strength to the utmost of your power, including steeds of war, to **strike terror into (the hearts of) the enemies**, of God and your enemies, and others besides, whom ye may not know, but whom God doth know. Whatever ye shall spend in the cause of God, shall be repaid unto you, and ye shall not be treated unjustly"*

Quran 3:151: *"Soon shall we **cast terror into the hearts of the Unbelievers**, for that they joined companions with God, for which He had sent no authority: their abode will be the Fire: And evil is the home of the wrong-doers!"*

Quran 8:16: 1 "***If any do turn his back to them*** *on such a day - unless it be in a stratagem of war, or to retreat to a troop (of his own)-* **he draws on himself the wrath of God, and his abode is Hell,** *- an evil refuge (indeed)!"*

Quran 9:39: those Muslim men **who refuse to fight and kill kafirs will be sent to hell**.

Teaching 8:16 allows **Muslim men who kill kafirs to avoid hell.**

Quran 3:169-170 allow **martyrs to go directly from life to paradise**, *where they wait for those Muslim men who must first go through the Day of Judgment.*

Quran 47:4:"Therefore, if it had been Allah's Will, He could certainly have exacted retribution from them (Himself); but (He lets you fight) in order to test you, some with others. But **those who are slain in the Way of Allah**, *- He will never let their deeds be lost."*

Islamic Heaven

Islamics don't have a heaven like Christians think. Just imagine a RELIGION that has as its place of holiness actually a place of debauchery. Just think about how God will get these people to worship him by having them continuously have sex. Rather than trying to convince you that the entire religion is on the subject of men being able to have sex if they kill people, here are a FEW of the verses.

Quran 2:25: *"And give glad tidings to those who believe and do righteous good deeds, that for them will be Gardens under which rivers flow (Paradise) ---and they will be given these things in the same form but different in taste and they shall have therein <u>purified mates and wives and that they will have</u> abide therein forever".*

Quran 3:15 *"<u>Virgins await</u> those who enter paradise."*

Quran 4.57 *"<u>Virgins await</u> those who enter paradise. "*

Quran 37:40-48 *"Those of the right hand-how happy will be those of the right hand! ...Who will be <u>honored in the Garden of Bliss;</u> - "who fight in His cause and slay and are slain"* *"they will <u>sit with bashful, dark eyed virgins</u> as chaste as the sheltered eggs of ostriches."*

Quran 38:52 *"<u>Female companions await</u> those who enter the Gardens of Eden on the Day of Reckoning."*

Quran: 44:51-55: "As for the righteous (Muslims)...We shall wed them to <u>beautiful virgins with lustrous eyes</u>"

Quran 52:17 *"Verily, those who fear will be in Gardens and Delight. Enjoying the (bliss) which their Lord has provided, and their Lord saved them from the torment of the blazing Fire. 'Eat and drink with glee, because of what you used to do.' They will recline on Throne Couches arranged in ranks; and we shall <u>join them to beautiful female maidens with big, lustrous eyes.</u>"*

Quran 56:17-37 *"Those in the Garden will be <u>attended by immortal youths with wide, lovely eyes</u>"-- "And (there will be) <u>virginal females</u> with wide, lovely eyes (as wives for the pious)"-- "Unending, and unforbidden, exalted beds, and <u>maidens incomparable</u>. We have formed them in a distinctive fashion and <u>made them to grow a new growth.</u> We made them virgins - pure and undefiled, lovers, matched in age."* —*"we created the <u>virginal females</u> and <u>made them virgins</u>, loving companions for those on the right hand-."*

Quran 78:31 - 32 "Verily for those who follow us, there will be a fulfillment of your desires: enclosed Gardens, grapevines, voluptuous <u>full-breasted maidens of equal age,</u> and a cup full to the brim of wine. There they never hear vain discourse nor lying - a gift in payment - a reward from your Lord."

Quran 78: 33-34:"And <u>young full-breasted maidens of equal age,</u> and a full cup of wine."

These are certainly not the only ones that describe a sex crazed heaven for those who murder enough, rape enough, or emulate the actions of Mohammed enough. Other verses in the Quran—such 55:56-58, 55:70-77, describe the Paradise to be an alluring whorehouse. The only reasons for being a Moslem are to keep someone from killing you as an apostate and sex. This is a special type of endless sex so there are converts every day to this sex cult. Speaking of sex, let's see how the Jinns make out.

Jinns

The Jinn are beings that are similar to regular people with free will, living on earth in a world parallel to mankind, such that they are invisible and they are made from smokeless fire. The Arabic word Jinn is from the verb 'Janna' which means to hide or conceal. The origins of the Jinn can be traced from the Quran and Mohammed the Sunna. Evidently, these Jinns had sex with many women, but the special women of the Brothel Heaven will have been untouched EVEN by Jinns.

Quran 15:26-27: *The Moon God says: "Indeed we created man from dried clay of black smooth mud. And we created the Jinn before that from the smokeless flame of fire"* Thus the Jinn were created before man.

SaheehMuslim: *As for their physical origin, then the Prophet, may the mercy and blessings of God be upon him, has confirmed the above verse when he said:* <u>*"The Angels were created from light and the Jinn from smokeless fire."*</u>

Except for this weird "being made of Fire" stuff; like "normal" humans, the Jinn too are required to worship the moon God and follow Islam. Their purpose in life is the same as the other Islamics…

Quran 51:56: *The Moon God Said: "I did not create the Jinn and mankind except to worship Me."* Jinns can thus be Muslims or non-Muslims.

Quran 72:1-2: *"Say (O' Muhammad): It has been revealed to me that a group of Jinn listened and said; 'Indeed we have heard a marvelous Quran. It guides unto righteousness so we have believed in it, and we will never make partners with our lord'*

According to Mohammed's religion, in many aspects of their world, the Jinn are very similar to us. They eat and drink, they marry, have children and they die. The life span however, is far greater then ours. Like us, they will also be subject to a Final Reckoning by God the Most High. They will be present with mankind on the Day of Judgment and will either go to Paradise or Hell.

Jinn Capabilities

One of the powers of the Jinn is that they are able to take on any physical form they like. Thus, they can appear as humans, animals, trees, and anything else. Having the ability to possess and take over the minds and bodies of other creatures is also a power which the Jinn supposedly have utilized greatly over the centuries. This however, is something which has been prohibited to them as it is a great oppression to possess another being. Human possession is something which has always brought about great attention.

It is not only humans which are possessed, but also animals, trees and other objects. By doing this, the evil Jinn hope to make people worship others besides the moon God. The possession of idols is one way to do this. The good Moslem ones go to heaven, but it is not certain if they get women or not.

Jinn's In Heaven

Quran 55; 46 *"For him who lives in terror of his Lord are two Gardens containing delights: shade, two fountains flowing, and fruits in pairs. Reclining on carpets lined with silk brocade, fruits hanging low. In them virginal females desiring none but you, undeflowered by men or jinn. Is the reward of goodness aught but goodness?"*

Quran 55:58: *"Wherein both will be chaste females restraining their glances, with whom no man or jinn has had tamth before them." -"Then which of the blessings of your lord will you both (jinn and men) deny? (In beauty) they are like rubies and coral".*

Quran 55:62 *"And beside this, there are two other Gardens, rich green in color from plentiful watering. In them will be two springs, gushing forth, and fruits. And beautiful companions, virgins cloistered in pavilions, undefiled by men and jinn, reclining on green cushions and rich mattresses. Which of the favors of you Lord will you both deny?"*

Quran 55:70-77*: "In each there shall be virgins chaste and fair-.dark eyed virgins sheltered in their tents whom neither man or Jinn have touched before-"*

One cannot talk about Jinns without bringing up a special one named El-karineh.

El Karineh and the Jinn

Somewhat similar to the ancient Jewish texts concerning Adam's first wife, the Islamic ruler over the Jinn is named "El-Karineh". She became the mother of the Jinn, handed out forbidden wheat to Eve [Hawa], Adam's second wife. After the "good" children Hawa, some of her children were called the seed of devils [sons of El-Karineh]. Adam was no saint either and had got many children by female Jinns [daughters of El-Karineh]. The descendants of those unclean Invisible people [Jinns] were called afrits, rassad, ghouls, marids, and so on. While they were still people, mostly they try to harm mankind. One might assume the Islamics believe the "unbelievers" come from this group. Here is an excerpt from "Our Father Adam".

At the first Adam was male and female in one body, man on one side, woman on the other. In due time the female part separated from the male, and became a perfect woman; and the couple mated. The female refused to submit to the male, saying they were made of the same dust, and he had no right to order her about. So she was turned out of Paradise, and, <u>consorting with Iblìs [Islamic Satan], and became the mother of devils.</u> [She is called "El-Karìneh" by Islamics, Lilith by Middle Eastern Jews, and "El-Brûsha" by the Spanish Jews].

*She is the deadly enemy of all women, especially such as have recently become mothers. --When "El-Karìneh" had been driven from Paradise, **Allah** created our mother Hawa [Eve], out of one of Adam's ribs, which He had extracted* *from the latter whilst he slept. Adam and Hawa were very happy together till Iblis succeeded in getting back into Paradise concealed in the hollow of the serpent's fangs [This serpent was none other than El-Karineh]. Having entered the garden, Satan succeeded in persuading Hawa to eat of the forbidden fruit, which, according to some of the learned, was wheat. Adam, having been persuaded by his wife to share his offence, was, as a punishment, cast out of Paradise, together with Hawa, Iblis, and the serpent. He had, however, the sense to snatch up, and bring down to earth with him, an anvil, a pair of tongs or pincers, two hammers, and a needle. ----- Two hundred years elapsed before Adam and Hawa met once more -----*

No! I do not know what the anvil, tongs, hammers, and needle were for, but it gives you a bid's eye view of the Mystic "religion" we are discussing.

Heaven for Sodomy?

The Quran seems to talk against homosexuality, but these verses seem strange. It appears, the lustful prophet came up with something for all who will kill for his Moon God. Evidently, never-molested (virgin) young boys like pearls will be available in abundance in the Muslim paradise for the blessed Muslim men to engage in sodomy.

***Quran 52:21** "Those who believe and whose families follow them in Faith, to them shall We join their offspring: Nor shall We deprive them of their works: (Yet) each individual is in pledge for his deeds. [**Wives and children will be joined with husbands and fathers who are cavorting with virgins**] And We shall provide fruit and meat, anything they desire. There they shall pass from hand to hand a (wine) cup free of frivolity, free of all taint of vanity or cause of sin. Round about them will serve, to them, **young boy servants** of their own (handsome) as **well-guarded pearls**.*

***Quran 56:13** "A multitude of those from among the first, and a few from the latter, (will be) on couch-like thrones woven with gold and precious stones. Reclining, facing each other. Round about them **will (serve) boys of perpetual (freshness)**, of never ending bloom, with goblets, jugs, and cups (filled) with sparkling wine. **No aching of the head will they receive, nor suffer any madness, nor exhaustion**. And with fruits, any that they may select: and the flesh of fowls, any they may* *desire. And there will be fair females with big eyes, lovely and pure, beautiful ones, like unto hidden pearls, well-guarded in their shells as a reward for the deeds."*

*Quran 76:19 "Those in the Garden will be **waited on by immortal youths [boys], as beautiful as scattered pearls**."* --

For additional verses one can use. Surat 52:24, 56:17, and 76:19. Another thing to do would be to not even think this is what heaven is like.

Zodiac Confusion

If the zodiac could control things, your holy books would have you swear by them. Guess what. Islamics have a swear thing.

Quran 85:1 *"I swear by the Zodiacal Signs, woe to the makers of the pit of fire. Cursed were the people."*

This is strange in that the zodiacal signs are used to tell the future and that is forbidden.

Muslim 4:1211:5440- *"The salah (daily prayer) of whoever approaches a fortune teller and asks him about anything will not be accepted for forty days and nights*

This is because Allah is the only one that knows.

Al-Qur'an 6:59- *"And with Him are the keys to the ghayb [all that is hidden], none knows them but He and He knows whatever there is in [or on) the earth and the sea; not a leaf falls, but he knows it. There is not a grain in darkness of the earth nor anything fresh or day, but is written in a clear record."*

Al-Qur'an 27:65- *"Say: None in the heavens and the earth knows the ghayb (unseen) except Allah, nor can they perceive when they shall be resurrected."*

Abu Dawud 3:1095:3895-*"Whoever approaches an oracle or fortune teller has disbelieved in what was revealed to Muhammad."*

Astrology is totally against Islam, but reread the first verse and notice that it has a very high number meaning it out trumps the earlier saying so there is still a question concerning if Islamics are allow to use astrology or not.

Women Go To Hell

What of Muslim women? Are they to be serviced by studs with eternal erections for all eternity? No such luck. The fate for most Muslim women is to burn in the fires of hell for all eternity. The only possible chance for a Muslim woman to ascend to Paradise is to completely obey her husband and even then, her chances are very slim.

Bukhari: 2:18:161*:"I (Mohammed) have seen that **the majority of the dwellers of Hell-Fire were women**... they are ungrateful to their husbands and they are deficient in intelligence".*

Bukhari 7:62:125*: "I have seen that the majority of the dwellers of Hell were women... they are ungrateful to their husbands and they are deficient in intelligence"*

OK! Some Muslim women do enter heaven, but they will find a very bleak existence, for, according to Muhammad, they will spend eternity standing in the corners of Paradise, watching their husbands, fathers, brothers engaging in sexual orgies.

Quran 52:21 *"Those who believe and whose families follow them in Faith, to them shall we join their offspring: Nor shall* we deprive them of their works: (Yet) each individual is in pledge for his deeds. *[This is saying w***ives and children will be joined with husbands who are having sex with virgins.]** And we shall provide fruit and meat, anything they desire.*

Description of Hell

So what is this hell that most women have to go to??

Quran 56:41 *"But those of the left hand-how unhappy those of the left hand. [Wouldn't you know it? I'm left handed!!] They will be in the scorching hot wind and boiling water, under the shadow of thick black smoke, neither cool nor agreeable. ...They will be gathered together on a certain day which is predetermined. Then you, the erring and the deniers will eat Zaqqoom [a thorn tree]. Fill your bellies with it, and drink scalding water, <u>lapping it up like female camels</u> raging of thirst and diseased. Such will be their entertainment, their welcome on the Day of Doom...the welcome of boiling water and the entertainment of roasting in Hell. This is the ultimate truth."*

Bukhari: 76:537 *"The Prophet said, 'Allah will say, "Adam!" <u>"I am obedient</u> to your orders." Allah will say, "Bring out the people of the Fire." "How many are the people of the Fire?" Allah will say, "Out of every thousand take out <u>nine-hundred and ninety-nine</u> persons." At that time children will become hoary-headed and <u>every pregnant female will drop her load.</u> You will see the people as if they were drunk. Allah's punishment will be very severe.'"*

Quran 68:42 *"On the day when the great calamity of doom befalls them in earnest, and <u>they are ordered to prostrate</u>*

themselves, they will not. There shall be a severe affliction. Their eyes will be downcast, abasement stupefying them; ignominy will cover them. Seeing that they had been summoned beforehand to bow in adoration, while they were still whole and unhurt, they refused."

Quran 68:44 *"Then leave me alone with such as reject this Message and call our pronouncements a lie. Systematically by degrees, step by step, we shall punish them in ways they can not even imagine."*

Bukhari: 4:54:487*"The Prophet said, 'The Hell Fire is 69 times hotter than ordinary worldly fires.' So someone said to 'Allah's Apostle wouldn't this ordinary fire have been sufficient to torture the unbelievers?'"*

Quran 7:41 *"They shall have a bed on the floor of Hell and coverings of fire; this is how we reward them."*

Quran 87:12 *"They will be flung in to burn in the great Fire and be made to taste it's burning, in which they will then neither die nor live?"*

Quran 88:1 *"Has the narration reached you of the overwhelming calamity? Some faces that Day, will be humiliated, downcast, scorched by the burning fire, while they are made to drink from a boiling hot spring."*

Quran 47:15 *"Those who shall dwell forever in the Fire are given to drink boiling water that tears their bowels to pieces, and cutting their intestines to shreds."*

To go to this place you must do anything Mohammed did not. Where he was mean, being nice makes one go to Hell, Where he was nice, which wasn't often, being mean would send you to hell. When we were sexually depraved, not being the same would send you to hell. He was the Sunna or perfection. Some think many of his actions were criminal

Crimes Of Muhammad

You can't really say there were any crimes of Mohammed as he was the perfect man of the Moon God. While we think of some of these things as inappropriate, they are, essentially, required to attain perfection similar to Mohammed. Muhammad is regarded by all Muslims as the most perfect human being ever created. His moon God tells us he is perfect and his **Sunna** must be emulated by all Muslim men. Therefore, Muslim's must look at what Mohammed did and emulate his actions as closely as possible. This is a short list of the actions of the moon God's most perfect man and what ALL Muslims are to try to achieve.

He molested a six-year-old girl named Aisha [his niece]. One of her duties was to clean semen from Mohammed's clothes. The prophet would take a bath with her with her and have her take his penis and rub it down her thighs. Being a man of mercy, he did not penetrate her initially.

He raped a nine year old. When Aisha was nine they consummated the married. Mohammed completed his sexual advance and he advocated sex with very young girls.

He oppressed Muslim women. He required them to cover their faces. He made them bow their heads or look downward. He defined when wives could be beaten and with all that, he defined that <u>most women WILL go to Hell</u> forever.

He married his daughter–in–law. To do this he had to change some of his previous rules, but he really thought his son's wife was a looker so his son would just be out of luck.

He raped a retarded woman and even had sex with his **dead aunt**.

He captured women and raped them. He kept women as sex slaves. This perfect man bragged about having sex with <u>61 women,</u> many of them were raped. Of these 61, he only had eleven wives at one time. Those, he sexually abused, forced sex during their menstruation, mentally abused his wives.

He beheaded his enemies. He really seemed to enjoy this action and it became one of the major commands in his Quran. Somewhere between 600 and 900 Jewish men at the massacre of Banu Qurayza had their heads lopped off in the name of his Moon God. Some were as young as 13. All boys had to be stripped and if any pubic hair was noticed, they were beheaded.

He assassinated people for insulting him or Islam. He established totalitarian rule.

He ordered the extermination, torture and terrorization of kafirs. He instigated 60 massacres and personally participated in 27 of them.

It almost goes without saying he was a slave trader. He owned and sold slaves which included enslaved women and children.

He hated Black people. He called his black slaves pug noses and compared them to Satan. It seems very strange to me that there are so many black Moslems today. What are they thinking???? When he had black slaves, he treated them like beasts of burden.

Terror was his middle name. He encouraged the rape of women in front of their husbands and if someone didn't pray when required, he would have them burned alive in their home. He personally committed acts of terror and advocated suicide attacks that he decided he should not do

He murdered prisoners of war, apostates, and homosexuals. Then he came up with honor killings of Muslim women and children. He ordered the murder, torture, terrorization of Christians and Jews if they did not convert to Islam.

He stoned adulators to death. He personally stoned a woman to death after she had given birth.

Here are a few of the important verses

Al-Anbiya' 21:107.-Allah says, "And we have not sent you [Mohammed] but as a mercy to the worlds."

Quran 33:21-"Ye have indeed in the Apostle of God a beautiful pattern of conduct for any one whose hope is in God and the Final Day, and who engages much in the Praise of God."

Quran 68:4"And verily, you (Muhammad) are on an exalted standard of character."

Mohammed's Actions

Here are a few of the things Islam is asking their people to do in their efforts to be like Mohammed.

Bukhari 882:795: "The Prophet cut off the hands and feet of the men belonging to the tribe of Uraina and did not cauterize (their bleeding limbs) till they died."

Bukhari 38:4474: "I saw the Apostle of Allah .... A man who had drunk wine was brought and he ordered them to beat him. So they beat him with what they had in their hands. Some struck him with whips, some with sticks and some with sandals. The <u>Apostle of Allah threw some dust on his face.</u>"

Ishaq: 676 " [A girl wrote]'You obey a stranger who encourages you to murder for booty. You are greedy men. Is there no honor among you?' Upon hearing those lines Muhammad said, 'Will no one rid me of this woman?' Umayr, a zealous Muslim, decided to execute the Prophet's wishes. That very night he crept into the writer's home while she lay sleeping surrounded by her young children. There was one at her breast. Umayr removed the suckling babe and then plunged his sword into the poet. The next morning in the mosque, Muhammad, who was aware of the assassination, said, 'You have helped Allah and His Apostle.' Umayr said. 'She had five sons; should I feel guilty?' 'No,' the Prophet answered. 'Killing her was as meaningless as two goats butting heads.'"

After having created his own god Allah, Muhammad utilized fake teachings from Allah to justify his crimes. Again, these criminal acts are not crimes in Islam but are the Sunna of Muhammad to be emulated by all Muslim men. Following is just a sample of Muhammad crimes recorded in the Hadith being sanctified by Allah [AKA Muhammad] in the Quran.

Child Molesting Sunna

Pedophilia in the Moslem community is a requirement rather than disgust. Muhammad molested his child wife Aisha at 6 and raped her when she was 9. His moon God not only divinely sanctioned this molestation but happily granted all Muslim men the divine right to molest and rape Muslim baby girls forever go try to achieve Mohammed's Sunna [Perfection]. The Adventures of his baby wife were renowned and talked about repeatedly.

Bukhari *claims that Muhammad married his wife Aisha when she was 6 and consummated the marriage at 9.*

Muslim *says that Aisha was 6 or 7 when Muhammad married her and she was 9 when taken to his house as his bride.*

The Dawud *collection states Aisha was 6 when married and that she had her first period when she was 9, at which point Muhammad had sex with her.*

Sunan an-Nasa'I *says that Aisha was 9 years old when Muhammad consummated their marriage.*

Sunan Ibn Majah *says that Aisha was 6 when married to Muhammad and 9 when that marriage was consummated.*

Mohammed's Other Baby Desires

Muslim 8:3460: - *[Muhammad posed this question] "Why didn't you marry a young girl so that you could sport with her and she could sport with you, or you could amuse with her and she could amuse with you?"*

In "The Life of Muhammad", we find an account in which Muhammad expressed a marital interest in a crawling baby. This event possibly occurred around the time of the Battle of Badr which would have made Muhammad approximately 55 years old. He had married Aisha two years earlier, when he was 53 years of age.

Suhayli 2:79: "I recorded that the apostle saw her when she was a baby crawling before him and said, 'If she grows up and I am still alive I will marry her.'

The Life of Muhammad: Muhammad saw Um Habiba the daughter of Abbas while she was at the age of nursing and he said, "If she grows up while I am still alive, I will marry her."

Muhammad in the Bathe

Bukhari 6:298 - Muhammad would take a bath with the little girl and fondle her.

Narrated by Aisha: "The Prophet and I used to take a bath from a single pot while we were Junub. During my period, he used to order me to put on an Izar (dress worn below the waist) and used to fondle me. While in Itikaf, he used to bring his head near me and I would wash it while I used to be in my periods."

Baby Aisha Work

Bukhari 4:232 – *Muhammad's wives would wash semen stains out of his clothes, which were still wet from the spot-cleaning even when he went to the mosque for prayers.*

Bukhari 1:4: 231*: "I asked 'Aisha about the clothes soiled with semen. She replied, "I used to wash it off the clothes of Allah's Apostle and he would go for the prayer while water spots were still visible."*

Fondling on Period

This seems to be one of his kinky desires that were considered SUNNA to be duplicated by the other Islamic hordes.

Dawud: 11: 2161*:"I and the Apostle of Allah used to lie in one cloth at night while I was menstruating. If anything from me smeared him, he washed the same place, and did not wash beyond it. If anything from him smeared his clothe, he washed the same place and did not wash beyond that, and prayed with it."*

Bukhari 6:300 - *Muhammad's wives had to be available for the prophet's fondling even when they were having their menstrual period.*

Bukhari 1:6:299*: (on the authority of his father) 'Aisha said: "Whenever Allah's Apostle wanted to fondle anyone of us during her periods, he used to order her to put on an Izar and start fondling her." 'Aisha added, "None of you could control his sexual desires as the Prophet could."*

Muslim I: 590 *Aisha said: "If anyone of us was having her menstrual period, Allah's Messenger ordered her to come to* him for sexual intercourse while she is on the peak of her period."

Maymuna: "The Messenger of Allah used to have sexual intercourse with me during my menstrual period, while a piece of garment is between us."

Don't Marry too Young

Quran 65:4 *says: "And those of your women as have passed the age of monthly courses, for them the 'Iddah (prescribed divorce period), if you have doubts (about their periods), is three months, and for those who have no courses (They are still immature if they skip too many periods) -- whosoever fears Allah and keeps his duty to Him, He will make his matter easy for him."*

Quran 65:4 clearly approves marriages and sexual copulation with pre-pubescent little girls, who haven't started continuous menstruating yet. And Muhammad at the age of 50 duly complied with this sanction of Allah by marrying his niece Aisha, only 6 years old, but held off on sex until she was 9. .

Extermination Sunna

Mohammed wasn't just child's play. His Sunna could be emulated other ways. Here is his Extermination Sunna.

Prisoners Should be Killed

Bukhari 5:59:448: "So Allah's Apostle went to them (i.e. besieged the Banu Quraiza). They then surrendered to the Prophet's judgment unconditionally after 25 days of fierce resistance but he directed them to Sad to give his [Mohammed's] verdict concerning them. Sad said, "I give my judgment that their warriors should be killed, their women and children should be taken as captives, and their properties distributed. "The Prophet said, "You have judged according to Allah's judgment." Hadith 447:5- The sentence: Death by decapitation for around 600 men and pubescent boys, and enslavement for the women and children.

Ibn Ishaq: 464 -says that the number may have been as high as 800—900.

Quran-8:17—"It is not ye who Slew them [the surrendered soldiers]; it is God; when you threw a handful of dust, it was not Thy act, but God's....."

Quran-8:67-"*It is not for any prophet to have captives until he hath made slaughter in the land. Ye desire the lure of this world and Allah desires the Hereafter, and Allah is Mighty, Wise.*" *(Allah insisting Prophet to kill all the prisoners, and should not keep any surrendered prisoners alive until He (Prophet) occupied entire Arabia.)*

Terrorism Sunna

Muhammad was the first of many Islamic terrorist s trying to emulate the Sunna [perfectness] of Mohammed.

Bukhari: 4:52:220-"*Allah's Apostle said, 'I have been made victorious with terror.'*

Quran 8:60 - "*Against them make ready your strength to the utmost of your power, including steeds of war, to strike terror into the hearts of the enemies, of God and your enemies, and others besides, whom ye may not know, but whom God doth know. Whatever ye shall spend in the cause of God, shall be repaid unto you, and ye shall not be treated unjustly*"

Quran 2.216: *Fighting is prescribed for Muslims.*

Quran 9:39:"*If you march not forth, He will punish you with a painful torment and will replace you with another people, and you cannot harm Him at all, and Allah is able to do all things.*"

Suicide Sunna

While Mohammed didn't have to really do this Suicide stuff, he talked about it being one of his Sunnas so let's see what is written.

Bukhari 52:54 - *The words of Muhammad: "I would love to be martyred in Allah's cause and then get resurrected and then get martyred, and then get resurrected again and then get martyred and then get resurrected again and then get martyred."*

Muslim 20:4678 - *During the battle of Uhud, Muhammad was desperate to push men into battle. He promised paradise for those who would martyr themselves, prompting a young man who was eating dates to throw them away and rush to his death.*

Muslim 20:4655 - *A man asks Muhammad "which of men is the best?" Muhammad replies that it is the man who is always ready for battle and flies into it "seeking death at places where it can be expected.*

Quran 4:74- *"Let those fight in the cause of God Who sell the life of this world for the hereafter. To him who fighteth in the cause of God, - whether he is slain or gets victory - Soon shall we give him a reward of great (value?*

Sex Slave Sunna

Mohammed's Slave Sunna included gang raping and similar things to be emulated. To preserve their worth coitus interuptus is also taught in their Biblical texts.

Bukhari 34:432 – This is another account of females taken captive and raped with Muhammad's approval. In this case, it is evident that the Muslims intended on selling the women after raping them because they are concerned about devaluing their price by impregnating them.

Sunan Abu Dawud 1:2166*: Narrated AbuSa'id al-Khudri: "A man said: Apostle of Allah, I have a slave-girl and I withdraw the penis from her (while having intercourse), and I dislike that she becomes pregnant. I intend (by intercourse) what the men intend by it. The Jews say that withdrawing the penis is burying the living girls on a small scale. He (the Prophet) said: The Jews told a lie. If Allah intends to create it, you cannot turn it away."*

Quran 4:3*- you fear that you will not act justly towards the orphans, marry such women as seem good to you, two, three, four; but if you fear you will not be equitable, then only one, or what your right hands own; so it is likelier you will not be partial.*

Bukhari 62:137 - *An account of women taken as slaves in battle by Muhammad's men after their husbands and fathers* were killed. The women were raped with Muhammad's approval.

Quran 4:24-"And all married women are forbidden) unto you save those captives whom your right hand possess."

<u>Islamics are even required to have sex with the female captives in front of the husband slaves.</u>

Sunan Abu Dawud: The Apostle of Allah sent a military expedition to Awtas on the occasion of the battle of Hunain. They met their enemy and fought with them. They defeated them and took them captives. Some of the companions of the Apostle of Allah were reluctant to have intercourse with the female captives in the presence of their husbands who were unbelievers.

Women Inferiority

I Mohammed though most women should go to hell, All Islamic must believe it. After all; Men are better than women. Generally, if the husband was not beating her, he is lording over her and she must live by a special set of rules to stay away from the whip. The concept of Wife rape does not exist in Islam. Muslim women are just property of Muslim men and even when they suffer so; they still will generally go to hell.

Bukhari 60:282 - *After Muhammad issued the command for women to cover themselves, the women responded by tearing up sheets to cover their faces.*

Abu Dawud 2:641: – *"The Prophet said: 'Allah does not accept the prayer of a woman who has reached puberty unless she wears a veil.'"*

Bukhari 52:250: - *"The Prophet said" "It is not permissible for a man to be alone with a woman, and no lady should travel except with a Muhram (male family member.)." - Neither is a woman allowed to travel by herself.*

Bukhari 60:51: *Jews used to say: "If one has sexual intercourse with his wife from the back, then she will deliver a squint-eyed child." So this Quran was revealed:*

Quran 2:223: *"Your wives are a tilth unto you; so go to your tilth when or how you will."*

Bukhari 4.54.460: Muhammad said: "If a husband calls his wife to his bed and she refuses and causes him to sleep in anger, the angels will curse her till morning." --

Ibn Majah 1854: "By him in Whose Hand lies my life, a woman cannot carry out the right of her Lord, till she carries out the right of her husband. And if he asks her to surrender herself [to him for sexual intercourse] she should not refuse him even if she is on a camel's saddle."

Quran 2:228- Men are "a degree" above women.

Quran 2:282- A woman is worth one-half a man.

Quran 37:22-23- "And it is said unto the angels: Assemble those who did wrong, together with their wives (even if they "behaved"), and what they used to worship."

Bukhari 6:301:"[Muhammad] said, 'Is not the evidence of two women equal to the witness of one man?' They replied in the affirmative. He said, 'This is the deficiency in her intelligence.'"

Women Are Dirty

Quran 4:43 "Muslims, draw not near unto prayer...(if) ye have touched women...then go to high clean soil and rub your face and your hands." (Muslim women are pariahs and dirty)."

Quran 5:6: - "When it's time to pray and you have just used the toilet or touched a woman, be sure to wash up. If you can't find any water, just rub some dirt on yourself."

Abu Dawud 2:704: - "...the Apostle of Allah said: When one of you prays without a sutrah, a dog, an ass, a pig, a Jew, a Magian, and a woman cut off his prayer, but it will suffice if they pass in front of him at a distance of over a stone's throw."

Women are Hell bound

Sahih Muslim 36: 6600: *Among the inmates of Heaven women will be the minority"*

Sahih Bukhari: 2:18:161 *"I (Mohammed) have seen that... [Because] they are ungrateful to their husbands and they are deficient in intelligence";*

Sahih Bukhari: 62:125:-- *the majority of the dwellers of Hell-Fire were women--*

Sahih Bukhari: 6:301:-- *the majority of the dwellers of Hell-Fire were women--*

Sahih Muslim 36: 6600:*"Among the inmates of Heaven women will be the minority"*

Ishaq: 185 *"In hell I saw women hanging by their breasts. They had fathered bastards."*

Women Are Stupid

Tabri: I: 280 'Allah said, "It is My obligation to make Eve bleed once every month as she made this tree bleed. I must also make Eve stupid, although I created her intelligent. Because Allah afflicted Eve, all of the women of this world menstruate and are stupid.

Sahih Bukhari: 2:18:161 "I (Mohammed) have seen that the majority of the dwellers of Hell-Fire were women... [Because] they are ungrateful to their husbands and they are deficient in intelligence"

.

Wife Beating

The Pakistan Institute of Medical Science has determined that over 90 percent of Pakistani Wives had been beaten or abused sexually, but don't' think they didn't deserve it. Some had made a bad meal while many of the others had not produced a male child. When not making the wrong meal or baby, Muslim Women Are Sex Objects for Men's Enjoyment. Here is some of the law that helps the Islamic husband to control his wives.

Muslim 4:2127 - *Muhammad struck his favorite wife, Aisha, in the chest one evening when she left the house without his permission. Aisha narrates, "He struck me on the chest which caused me pain."*

Remember ANYTHING Mohammed did is considered what is needed to become perfect.

Bukhari 7:72:715- A woman came to Muhammad and begged her to stop her husband from beating her. Her skin was bruised so badly that she it is described as being "greener" than the green veil she was wearing. Muhammad did not admonish her husband, but instead ordered her to return to him and submit to his sexual desires.

Abu Dawud 2142- "The Prophet said: A man will not be asked as to why he beat his wife."

***Bukhari 7:62:132**-* The Prophet said, "None of you should flog his wife as he flogs a slave and then have sexual intercourse with her in the last part of the day." *(Ideally when you flog one of your wives, let her recuperate that day and sleep with your other wives or your slave girls.)*

Quran: 4:34 *"Men are the maintainers of women because Allah has made some of them to excel others and because they spend out of their property; the good women are therefore obedient, guarding the unseen as Allah has guarded; and those on whose part you fear desertion, admonish them, and leave them alone in the sleeping-places and <u>beat them</u>; then if they obey you, do not seek a way against them; surely Allah is High, Great."*

Four Wives Law

Men can marry up to four women if they treat them equally; unlimited forcible concubine rape is also permitted and encouraged, especially if you think you might like one over another. Not only are men allowed to practice polygamy, but they may also capture women in war and use them as sex slaves. This is considered morally legitimate according to the Quran. In other words, non-Muslim women have no right to be free from the horror of slavery and serial rape by Muslim men. Note the term "whom your right hand possess" means slaves. It is known that Mohammed's right hand owned dozens of sex slaves.

Quran 4.24: " *(prohibited are) women already married, except <u>those whom your right hands possess</u>: Thus hath Allah ordained (Prohibitions) against you: Except for these, all others are lawful, provided ye seek them in marriage with gifts from your property,- desiring chastity, not lust, <u>seeing that ye derive benefit from them</u>, give them their dowers as prescribed; but if, after a dower is prescribed, agree Mutually, there is no blame on you, and Allah is All-knowing, All-wise."*

Quran 4:3 *"Marry women of your choice, Two or three or four; but if ye fear that ye shall not be able to deal justly with them, then only one [wife is allowed], [If you think you want one over another then just use salves] or (a captive) that your right hands possess, that will be more suitable, to prevent you from doing injustice."*

Quran 4:25 *"If any of you have not the means wherewith to wed free believing women, they may wed believing girls from among those whom your right hands possess."*

Only have sex with the multitude of wives or Slaves.

Quran 23.1-6: *"Successful indeed are the believers, who are humble in their prayers, and who keep aloof from what is vain, and who are givers of poor-rate, and who guard their private parts, except before their mates or those whom their right hands possess, for they surely are not blameable."*

This is the Quran which gives the slave owner the right of sexual access to his female slaves. The term "guarding the private parts" is a synonym for sexual intercourse.

Try not to sells your slaves into Prostitution

The Quran not only allows slavery and sex with captured women and slave girls, it says God may even pardon those who forced their slave girls to sell their bodies.

Quran 24.33: *"Force not your slave-girls to whoredom that ye may seek enjoyment of the life of the world, if they would preserve their chastity. And if one force them, then (unto them), after their compulsion, lo! Allah will be Forgiving, and Merciful. He said that this is not blameable if indulges with wives and slaves."*

Quran 70: 29-35 *"And those who guard their private parts, Except in the case of their wives or those whom their right hands possess -- for these surely are not to be blamed, But he* *who seeks to go beyond this, these it is that go beyond the limits -- And those who are faithful to their trusts and their covenant And those who are upright in their testimonies, And those who keep a guard on their prayer, Those shall be in gardens, honored."*

Mohammed Needed More Wives

Muhammad couldn't stand it and wanted to marry his son-in-law's wife which would mean he had too many waives so he came up with a new law.

Quran 33:50-52 *"O Prophet! We have made lawful to thee thy wives to whom thou hast paid their dowers; and those whom thy right hand possesses out of the prisoners of war whom God has assigned to thee; and daughters of thy paternal uncles and aunts, and daughters of thy maternal uncles and aunts, who migrated with thee; and any believing woman who dedicates her soul to the Prophet if the Prophet wishes to wed her;-* **this only for thee**, *and not for the Believers (at large); We know what We have appointed for them as to their wives and the captives whom their right hands possess;- in order that there should be no difficulty for thee. And God is Oft- Forgiving, Most Merciful. Thou mayest defer any of them that thou pleasest, and thou mayest receive any thou pleasest: and there is no blame on thee if thou invite one whose (turn) thou hadst set aside. This were nigher to the cooling of their eyes, the prevention of their grief, and their satisfaction - that of all of them - with that which thou hast to give them: and God knows (all) that is in your hearts: and God is All-Knowing, Most Forbearing. It is not lawful for thee (to marry more) women after this, nor to change them for (other) wives, even though their beauty attract thee, except any thy right hand should possess (as handmaidens): and God doth watch over all things."*

Allah graciously allowed Muslims to own and rape slave girls. Prophet Muhammad himself and his disciples routinely raped their slave girls. Muslim men were permitted unlimited raping of their slaves and even gang rape. Sex slaves were one of the main factors in the spread of Islam.

What of those Muslim women who are raped?

More Women Stuff

Here is some interesting Fatwa and Sharia Law items concerning women.

Fatwa 13814:12:150-Women are not permitted to attend universities where both men and women are taught or all-female schools with male teachers.

Fatwa 667:17:142-150- Women over the age of puberty are not permitted to leave the house without covering the body (except face and hands).

Fatwa 2501:1:429- Women are not permitted to visit the graves of loved ones.

Fatwa 2595:1:719- Women are not permitted to obtain passports (since their photographs in them may tempt men), unless for the purpose of making Hajj (pilgrimage to Mecca).

Fatwa 12139:11:38- Women are not permitted to travel without a spouse or male relative.

Fatwa 9693: 12:381-Women are not permitted to be alone with men who are not relatives or spouses, and the punishment for such "indecency" is whipping or stoning.

Fatwa 9693:12:382- Women are not permitted to speak softly to a man or otherwise provoke his desire with letters, *phone calls or glances, the <u>punishment of which is whipping or stoning</u>.*

Sharia m3:.13*-Young women may be forced to marry without their consent to total strangers.*

Sharia m10:12*- A husband may beat his wife and confine her to the house*

Sharia m6.10*- A husband can divorce a wife at will*

Sharia n3:2*- A husband can marry multiple wives*

Sharia m13:4-5*- and he automatically gets custody of children at age 7 or if the mother remarries*

Sharia o8.7:19*-Worse yet, women are forced to abide by Sharia Law rulings against them because challenging rulings of the "Lawgiver" is an act of apostasy, punishable by death.*

OK! Women are less than men, a play thing, and one who must reverence her husband and still go to Hell, but is there something sinister about the religion??? This next thing may give us a clue.

Female Genital Mutilation

Here is a great Moslem tradition. Cutting out the clitoris, cutting off pieces of the Labia Majora and Minor, and sewing a girl together such that a small straw is inserted in the vaginal opening as a girl's legs are tied together while the tiny opening insures by the operation allows the parents to insure chastity of their girls. I know you think this is barbaric, but more than 125 million girls and women **alive today** have been "cut" in the 29 countries in Africa and Middle East alone. To make it sound "respectable", the Islamics and their "Bible" call it Circumcision. Let me just call it FGM. This Muslim atrocity is mostly carried out on young girls sometime between infancy and age 15. Just imagine having to go through something like this at the age of 15!

Don't think that this only happens where Islam is a "required religion". According to the Centers for Disease Control and Prevention, at least 150,000 to 200,000 girls in the U.S. have probably been forced to undergo FGM and the number is on the rise as immigrant numbers from Africa and Moslem countries is skyrocketing. Certainly, it is against the law to do something like this in the U.S, but Muslims would simply "go on vacation" and bring back a less happy child.

As immigration to the U.S. from countries in Africa quadrupled between 1990 and 2011 from 360,000 to 1.6 million, you can imagine how fast the number is increasing. Luckily, some of the practitioners have realized the shame. One "cutter", Amran Mohamud, 40, spent 15 years cutting girls. She remembers the girls who wouldn't stop bleeding. She remembers the infections that set in. Four years ago, she abandoned the trade after a religious leader convinced her it should not be an Islamic tradition. Luckily, she did not read the Koran often and was fooled. Here is what "The Reliance of the Traveler", a respected manual of Shafi'i jurisprudence and the Quran, says about the barbaric "REQUIREMENT".

The Reliance of the Traveler-*"Circumcision is obligatory for every male and female by cutting off the piece of skin on the glans of the penis of the male, but circumcision of the female is by cutting out the clitoris"*

Quran 4:11- *Circumcision (Female Genital Mutilation) is "obligatory" for women.*

What Is Genital Mutilation?

The age of the girls varies from weeks after birth to puberty; in half the countries for which figures were available in 2013, luckily, most girls were cut before the age of five.

The practice involves one or more of several procedures, including removal of all or part of the clitoris and clitoral hood; all or part of the clitoris and inner labia; and in its most severe form something called infibulation, where all or part of the inner and outer labia and the closure of the vagina. For infibulation, a small hole is left for the passage of urine and menstrual blood, and the vagina must be opened up for intercourse and childbirth.

The practice is an ethnic marker, rooted in gender inequality, ideas about purity, modesty and aesthetics, and attempts to control women's sexuality.

For the Clitorectomy portion, "the clitoris is held between the thumb and index finger, pulled out and amputated with one stroke of a sharp object. Bleeding is usually stopped by packing the wound with gauzes or other substances and applying a pressure bandage. Modern trained practitioners may insert one or two stitches around the clitoral artery to stop the bleeding"

Iinfibulation

For infibulation, we are talking about the removal of all external genitalia and **the fusing of the wound**, leaving a small hole (about an inch) for the passage of urine and menstrual blood. The inner and outer labia are cut away, with or without excision of the clitoris. A pinhole is created by inserting something into the wound before it closes, such as a twig or rock salt. The wound may be sutured with surgical thread or agave or acacia thorns may be used to hold the sides together; according to a 1982 study in Sudan, eggs or sugar might be used as an adhesive. The girl's legs are then tied from hip to ankle for 2–6 weeks until the tissue has bonded. To let you know just how wide spread this "custom" is , in Somalia 98 percent of women affected, Guinea (96 percent), Djibouti (93 percent), Egypt (91 percent), Eritrea (89 percent), Mali (89 percent), Sierra Leone (88 percent), Sudan (88 percent), Gambia (76 percent), Burkina Faso (76 percent), Ethiopia (74 percent), Mauritania (69 percent), Liberia (66 percent), and Guinea-Bissau (50 percent).

Outside Africa FGM has significant use in Yemen, Iraq, Indonesia and Malaysia, India, UAE, Colombia, Oman, Peru Sri Lanka, Jordan and Saudi Arabia. Additionally, immigrant communities in Australia, New Zealand, Europe,

Scandinavia, the United States and Canada add to this attack on sanity by the Islamic "CULT".

Reasons for continuing this barbaric show of male superiority includes curbing premarital sex, reducing a woman's sexual desire so that her husband can more easily take several wives. In both cases, they argue, the aim is to serve the interests of male sexuality. It is praised in several *hadith* (sayings attributed to Muhammad) as noble. In 2006, there was an outward proclamation to end the practice, but it is believed that several countries, particularly Eritrea, Egypt, Guinea, Mali and Mauritania, still push this nastiness as a religious requirement.

Murder For Dishonor

Dishonoring a Muslim man is a grave crime, deserving murder. A Muslim man defines his honor not by his own integrity and dignified actions, but through the actions and behaviors of his wife and children who are his property.

Honor murder is sanctioned in "Umdat al-Saliq" or "Reliance of the Traveler", a manual of Islamic law, certified in 1991 as a reliable guide to Sunni Islam by Cairo's al-Azhar University, the most prestigious and authoritative institute of Sunni Islamic jurisprudence in the world. This 14th-century law-manual states the following about punishment.

Section 1.1-2: *"Retaliation is obligatory against anyone, who kills a human being purely intentionally and without right",* EXCEPT when *"a father or mother (or their fathers or mothers)" kills their "offspring, or offspring's offspring"*

In other words, a parent, who murders his/her child for the sake of honor, is not a crime under Islamic law or Shariah.

Grand Ayatollah Ruhollah Khomeini *(1902-1989) the supreme authority of Shiite Islam gave immunity for parents, who murder their children. In his book, "Resaleh Towzih Al-Massael" there is no penalty for a father who kills his child. A killer is punished only if: "The slayer is not the father of the slain, or the parental grandfather".*

Flog For Fornication Even to Death

For this, you must understand that a death sentence by flogging was 40 lashes. Many of the Bible heroes had been flogged as much as 39 times to be on the brink of death. There is no doubt that a punishment of 100 lashes was to be a punishment of death with an occasional person who survives accidentally. If Muslims are to follow the Quran, they have to mercilessly flog lovers 100 times, if they make love before marriage. I know this almost sounds like a righteous cult, but listen what the salve owner/ trader/sex assaulter Mohammed allowed if the raping is of an outsider, sex slave, or possession.

Quran 24:2: *"The woman and the man guilty of adultery or fornication, - <u>flog each of them with a hundred stripes</u>: Let not compassion move you in their case, in a matter prescribed by God, if ye believe in God and the Last Day: and let a party of the Believers witness their punishment."*

Quran Encourages Slave Sex

Muslims are encouraged to live in the way of Muhammad, who was a slave owner and trader. He captured slaves in battle; had sex with his slaves; and instructed his men to do the same. The Quran devotes more verses to making sure that Muslim men know they can keep women as sex slaves than it does to telling them to pray five times a day. Many pray 5 times so we can be sure they try their best to have sex slaves properly worked. This horrible crime of serial rape against a non-Muslim woman is not considered adultery or fornication. Instead, <u>it is a divinely sanctified virtuous act.</u> Sharia law is dedicated to the practice getting and using sex slaves. Here are a few examples.

Quran 33:50:- *"O Prophet! We have made lawful to thee thy wives to whom thou hast paid their dowers; and those (slaves) whom thy right hand possesses out of the prisoners of war whom <u>Allah has assigned to thee</u>"*

Even their Moon God wants them to use the slaves for sex. While Muslims are restrained to four wives, following the example of their prophet, they are SUPPOSED TO have sex with any number of slaves.

Quran 23:5-6 and 70:29-30:- *"...who abstain from sex, except with those joined to them in the marriage bond, or (the captives) whom their right hands possess..."*

Quran 4:24: - *"And all married women (are forbidden unto you) save those (captives) whom your right hands possess."*

If you own a slave, her marriage means nothing to the Islamic.

Quran 8:69-71: - *"But <u>"enjoy"</u> what ye took in war, lawful and good" --"Allah gave you mastery over them."*

A reference to war booty, of which slaves were a part; the Muslim slave master may enjoy his "catch"

Quran 24:32: - *"And marry those among you who are single and those who are fit among <u>your male slaves and your female slaves...</u>"*

This does not mean to let your slaves go to get married. It means breeding slaves based on fitness allowed for more "enjoyment".

Encouraged Slavery

While the Early Christians were enslaved and slavery was commonplace during the times when the Bible was written, there are no verses encouraging people to enslave others. Certainly, there were some sections of the Old Testament where slavery had been encouraged, but this writing was thousands of years after the Old Testament and well past the "new requirements of Brotherly love" in the New Testament writings. Anyway, here is what they believe

Bukhari 80:753: - *"The Prophet said, 'The freed slave belongs to the people who have freed him.'"*

Bukhari 52:255*: - The slave who accepts Islam and continues serving his Muslim master will receive a double reward in heaven.*

Bukhari 41.598: *-* <u>*Slaves are property.*</u> *They cannot be freed if an owner has outstanding debt, but can be used to pay off the debt.*

Bukhari 62:137*: - This is an account of women taken as slaves in battle by Muhammad's men after their husbands and fathers were killed. The women were raped with Muhammad's approval.*

Bukhari 34:432*: - This is an account of females taken captive and raped with Muhammad's approval. In this case, it is evident that the Muslims intended on <u>selling the women after raping them</u> because they are concerned about devaluing their price by impregnating them. .

Bukhari 47.765: - In this section, a woman is <u>rebuked by Muhammad for freeing a slave</u> girl. *The prophet tells her that she would have gotten a greater heavenly reward by giving her to a relative (as a slave).*

Mohammed Slave Trader

Why shouldn't the Quran and other books praise slavery? Mohammed was a great slave trader. OK! He kept a lot for sex, but many were sold by him. Here are some of the descriptions of his slaving.

Bukhari 34:351: *- Muhammad sells a slave for money. As a slave trader, this shows the type of prophet this man really was and he pushed his views of the Islamic super race to all who would listen.*

Bukhari 72:734*: - This is just one of many places in the Hadith where a reference is made to a human being owned by Muhammad. In this case, the slave is of African descent.*

Muslim 3901 *- Muhammad trades away two black slaves for one Muslim slave.*

Muslim 4112 *- A man freed six slaves on the event of his death, but Muhammad reversed the emancipation and kept four in slavery to himself. He cast lots to determine which two to free.*

Bukhari 47:743: *- Muhammad order the building of his pulpit - from which he preached Islamic requirements for slave and how much more superior his followers were.*

Ibn Ishaq 693: - *"Then the apostle sent Sa-d b. Zayd al-Ansari, brother of Abdu'l-Ashal with some of the captive women of Banu Qurayza to Najd and he sold them for horses and weapons."*

Muhammad trades away women captured from the Banu Qurayza tribe to non-Muslim slave traders for property. When talking about Mohammed, it should be noted that the men of the tribe where the women had come had been executed after surrendering peacefully without a fight).

Force Rape in Front of Husbands

I mentioned this before, but I think it needs repeating. Here is an overview that shows what is required of the Islam to become like Mohammed and gain entrance into the heaven of debauchery.

Rape in front of Husbands

Abu Dawud 2150: - *"The Apostle of Allah (May peace be upon him) sent a military expedition to Awtas on the occasion of the battle of Hunain. They met their enemy and fought with them. They defeated them and took them captives. Some of the Companions of the Apostle of Allah were reluctant to have intercourse with the female captives in the presence of their husbands who were unbelievers. So Allah, the Exalted, sent down the Quranic verse: (Quran 4:24) 'And all married women (are forbidden) unto you save those (captives) whom your right hands possess."* This is the background for Quran 4:24 of the Quran. Not only does Allah grant permission for women to be captured and raped, but allows it to even be done in front of their husbands. (See also Muslim 3432 & Ibn Kathir/Abdul Rahman Part 5 Page 14)

Amusing Beatings

Abu Dawud 1814 - "...[Abu Bakr] He then began to beat [his slave] him while Mohammed was smiling and saying: Look at this man who is in the sacred state " This section is about the future first caliph of Islam beating his slave for losing a camel while Muhammad looks on in amusement.

Ibn Ishaq 734: – In this section, a slave girl is given a "violent beating" by Ali in the presence of Muhammad, who does nothing about it.

Double Punishment if you Bleed Too Quickly

Abu Dawud 38:4458 - *Narrated Ali ibn AbuTalib: "A slave-girl belonging to the house of the Apostle of Allah committed fornication. He said: Rush up, Ali, and inflict the prescribed punishment on her. I then hurried up, and saw that blood was flowing from her, and did not stop. So I came to him and he said: Have you finished inflicting (punishment on her)? I said: I went to her while her blood was flowing. He said: Leave her alone till her bleeding stops; then inflict the prescribed punishment on her. And inflict the prescribed punishment on those whom your right hands possess (i.e. slaves)".* A slave girl is ordered by Muhammad to be beaten until she bleeds, and then beaten again after the bleeding stops. He indicates that this is prescribed treatment for slaves.

Women's Rights

This is a simple one. If people do not want women's rights, they should allow Sharia Law. If they do, we had better stop this insanity. Here is a tiny example

Quran 4:34: *"Men have authority over women because Allah has made the one superior to the other, and because they spend their wealth to maintain them. Good women are obedient. They <u>guard their unseen parts</u> because Allah has guarded them. As for those from whom you fear disobedience, admonish them and send them to beds apart and beat them."*

Besides having to put a bag over their head at all times in public, they must be completely obedient. Your wives must be separated and beaten. I think the major difference between slaves and Islamic wives is that they are beaten with a smaller stick and have fewer hits.

Retaliation Murder

Quran 2:178: - *"O ye who believe! Retaliation is prescribed for you in the matter of the murdered; the freeman for the freeman, and <u>the slave for the slave, and the female for the female.</u>"*

This is the Islamic rule of retaliation for murder. It means that more slaves must be killed to avenge a Muslim and if you are killing females, it takes even more.

Quran 16:71-75: --- *the owner should be careful about insulting Allah by bestowing Allah's gifts on slaves- - those whom the god of Islam has not favored "Allah sets forth the Parable (of two men: one) a slave under the dominion of another; He has no power of any sort; and (the other) a man on whom We have bestowed goodly favors from Ourselves, and he spends thereof (freely), privately and publicly: are the two equal? By no means; praise be to Allah."*

This specifically indicates that the moon God does not believe all are created equal. Instead, all slaves are made by the Moon God and should not be considered as people.

Murder By Stoning

This is a story about how different a man of the moon God is than Jesus teachings. Muhammad had a woman, who had conceived through adultery, stoned to death immediately after she gave birth. The following hadith describes the gruesome punishment:

Muslim, 4206: *"And when he had given command over her and she was put in a hole up to her breast, he ordered the people to stone her. Khalid b. al-Walid came forward with a stone which he threw at her head, and when the blood spurted on his face he cursed her..."*

Please notice that there is no similar stoning of her partner.

Murder for Not Praying

This commandment is not just killing someone for missing a prayer; it indicates that the prophet of the moon God commands that they be burned alive. While the person is burning, someone is commanded to lead a prayer.

Bukhari, 1.11.626: *"The Prophet said, "burn all those who had not left their houses for the prayer, burning them alive inside their homes."*

Bukhari, 1.11.617: *"I would order someone to collect firewood and another to lead prayer. Then I would burn the houses of men who did not present themselves at the compulsory prayer and prostration."*

Castration Extermination of Blacks

Sahih Moslem 9: 46-47: *In this Hadith, Muhammad is quoted as saying that Blacks are, "pug-nosed slaves". I don't understand what that means, but it sounds bad to me.*

Tabari II: 21: *"Ham [Africans] begat all those who are black and curly-haired, while Japheth [Turks] begat all those who are full-faced with small eyes, and Shem [Arabs] begat everyone who is handsome of face with beautiful hair.* <u>*Noah prayed that the hair of Ham's descendants would not grow beyond their ears, and that whenever his descendants met Shem's, the latter would enslave them.*</u>*"*

I know this doesn't sound like the Noah of the Bible, but it is a way to change the meaning of Biblical testimony. Certainly, Noah cursed Cainan because Ham laughed at him being drunk and naked, but that had to do with Cainan marrying outside his own clan as he married one of the Descendants of the ANAK. To the Islamic, black people are only deserving of being enslaved.

Ishaq: 243: *"I heard the Apostle say: 'Whoever wants to see Satan should look at Nabtal!' He was a black man with long* *flowing hair, inflamed eyes, and dark ruddy cheeks.... Allah sent down concerning him: 'To those who annoy the Prophet there is a painful doom."*

Quran 9:61: *"Gabriel came to Muhammad and said, <u>'If a black man comes to you his heart is more gross than a donkey's.</u>'"*

To reduce this affliction, Islamic cultists tried genocide by castration. Blacks, were enslaved by the Islamic Arabs, and castrated. The result is obvious: while most black slaves sent to the Americas and Europe could marry and have families, a larger number male Black slaves sent to the Middle East and other parts of the Islamic world, were all castrated, and the black populations of the Moslem world was reduced rather than flourished. It should be noted that a relatively large number of Black males died immediately from the unhygienic castration process.

It simply amazes me the number of Moslem converts that are black people.

Murder For Payment

Ibn Timiyya Vol. 32, p. 202: *"If an owned slave assaults somebody and damages his property, his crime will be tied to his neck. It will be said to his master, 'If you wish, you can pay the fine for the damages done by your slave or deliver him to be sentenced to death.' His master has to choose one of the two options – either the value of the slave and his price or the damage the slave has caused."*

So if you had your slave drive somewhere and there is an accident where a pile of wheat is damaged, the owner can simply have the slave killed. While this makes no sense at all, notice the person who lost his wheat does not get the slave. The slave can only be killed. The absurdity is amazing.

Murder Prisoners and Gays

Quran 8:67: *"It is not for any prophet to have captives until he hath made slaughter in the land. Ye desire the lure of this world and Allah desireth (for you) the Hereafter, and Allah is Mighty, Wise."*

The Moon God ordered killing before taking prisoners. Allah insisted that Mohammed should kill all prisoners, and should not keep any surrendered prisoners alive. This tactic of fear allowed Mohammed to take full control of Arabia.

Treatment of Gays

Abu Dawud, 4447: *'If you find anyone doing as Lot's people did, kill the one who does it, and the one to whom it is done'.*

Another hadith says that homosexuals should be burned alive or killed by pushing walls upon them:

Ibn Abbas and Abu Huraira reported God's messenger as saying, 'Accursed is he who does what Lot's people did.' In a version . . . on the authority of Ibn Abbas it says that Ali [Muhammad's cousin and son—in—law] had two people burned and that Abu Bakr [Muhammad's chief companion] had a wall thrown down on them. (Mishkat, vol. 1, p. 765, Prescribed Punishments)

Laws of Jihad

Essentially, there are no laws. Just anything, you can think of. The following are some of the legalized rules of Jihad found in the Quran, hadith, and classical legal opinions:

- **Women and children enslaved.** They can either be sold, or the Muslims may 'marry' the women, since their marriages are automatically annulled upon their capture. Muslim men can murder their slaves.
- **Jihadists may have sex with slave women.** Ali, Muhammad's cousin and son-in-law, did this. This is rape.
- **Kill women and children at night**-Women and children must not be killed during war, unless this happens in a nighttime raid when visibility was low. All those killed in Jihad are acts of Murder. To kill in the name of God is murder.
- **Old men and monks** could be killed.
- A captured enemy of war could be killed, enslaved, ransomed for money or an exchange, freely released, or beaten. One time Muhammad even tortured a citizen of the city of Khaybar in order to extract information about where the wealth of the city was hidden. When he refused

to reveal the location of the city wealth, he was taken and murdered by beheading.

- **Threat of Murder to force conversions-** Enemy men who converted could keep their property and small children. This law is so excessive that it amounts to forced conversion. Only the strongest of the strong could resist this coercion and remain a non-Muslim.
- **Civilian property** may be confiscated.
- **Civilian homes** may be destroyed.
- **Civilian fruit trees** may be destroyed.
- **Pagan Arabs had to convert** or die. This does not allow for the freedom of religion or conscience.
- **People of the Book** (Jews and Christians) had three options (Quran 9:29):
  - **Die**;
  - **Convert and** pay a forced 'charity' or zakat tax; Refusal or future failure to pay this tax meant your **murder**.
  - **Keep their Biblical faith** and pay a jizya or poll tax. Refusal or future failure to pay this tax meant your **murder**.

Crazy Music Laws

Muhammad had murdered poets, who criticized his actions and decreed that all music was to be destroyed from the human race. If we let it take over, Islam will destroy the joy of all music. I know you thought the killing of innocents was bad, but then the Sunna wants music to be outlawed.

Hadith Qudsi 19:5: *"The Prophet said that Allah commanded him to <u>destroy all the musical instruments</u>, idols, crosses and all the trappings of ignorance."*

Umdat al-Salik r40.0: "Allah Mighty and Majestic sent me as a guidance and mercy to believers and commanded me to <u>do away with musical instruments</u>, flutes, strings, crucifixes, and the affair of the pre-Islamic period of ignorance."

Umdat al-Salik "On the Day of Resurrection, Allah will <u>pour molten lead into the ears</u> of whoever sits listening to a songstress."

Umdat al-Salik "<u>Song makes hypocrisy grow</u> in the heart as water does herbage."

Umdat al-Salik "This community will experience the swallowing up of some people by the earth, metamorphosis of some into animals, and being rained upon with stones." Someone asked, "When will this be, O Messenger of Allah?" and he said, "<u>When songstresses and musical instruments appear</u> and wine is held to be lawful."

Umdat al-Salik *"There will be peoples of my Community who will hold fornication, silk, wine, <u>and musical instruments to be lawful</u> ...."*

The Ayatollah Khomeini: *"<u>Allah did not create man so that he could have fun</u>. The aim of creation was for mankind to be put to the test through hardship and prayer. An Islamic regime must be serious in every field. There are no jokes in Islam. There is no humor in Islam. There is no fun in Islam. There can be no fun and joy in whatever is serious."*

Inappropriate Laws

Many of the Islamic laws are inappropriate, but here are a few that I thought should be placed on the inappropriate pedestal. Murder in the Quran and Sunna of the prophet is reinforced in Sharia Law. Here we find out the horrible things to consider. Changing one's religion, mocking anything Mohammed said, criticizing Islam, and saying you like democracy are all punishable by DEATH. These are the epitome of Sharia law. My feeling is we should not allow Sharia Law to be used in America even if it is "holy".

Fatwa 4400, Part No. 1, Page 334 & 335: The punishment for changing or discarding one's Islamic religion is <u>death.</u>

Fatwa 2196, Part No. 2, Page 42: Mocking anything in the Quran or the Sunna of the prophet Muhammad is apostasy and therefore punishable by death.

Fatwa 21021, Part No. 1, Page 414: Criticizing Islam, shari'ah law or the Sunna of the prophet Muhammad is apostasy and therefore punishable by death.

Fatwa 19351, Part No. 22, Page 239-248: Any Muslim who states a preference for democracy rather than shari'ah law or questions anything in the Quran or Sunna is a Kafir (disbeliever of Islamic Cultism), considered an apostate, and therefore sentenced to death.

The Black Flag

No! I'm not talking about insecticide; I'm talking about the NEW flag, shown below.

Seems like many Moslems have gone away from the Moon God crescent flag to get what many call the flag of Al-Qaida or the flag of Jihad. Over the past few years, the black flag has been observed amidst the protests and riots in Egypt, Libya, Sudan, Nigeria, Lebanon, Jordan, Iraq, Syria, Kuwait, Bahrain, Iran, Pakistan, Bangladesh, Afghanistan, Indonesia, India, Turkey, Jerusalem, Gaza and even Germany, Australia and England. Across the world, Muslims of every race, tribe and nation are marching under the same black banner and burning our flag as shown below.

The picture shows protesters burn the U.S. flag under the black banner of Islam in London. May times the sword of Mohammed is below the insignia informing all that Allah is the only god and Mohammed is the most perfect person. It's such a great flag; it is flown over the U.S. Embassy in Tunisia as shown below.

It is believed that the symbol of the black flag belongs to terrorist groups and the Hizbut-Tahrir. Their goal is the take over of the world through non-violent means so that it can be controlled as a single Caliphate super state, led by a single leader, known as the Caliph. This Caliph would be equivalent to the pope, president and all leaders of the world, bringing the religious, governmental and military offices all under one head.

If we could just see the future, we could determine if this nationalism is anything for us to worry about. Luckily, there might be a way to see the future.

What About the Future?

Luckily or unluckily, people have seen and told us about our future. Many of those are fakes, but some have absolutely been correct in determining our future. In those prophecies, there is a common theme; Moslems will take over a large portion of the world very, very soon. The date is not specifically identified except that it will be soon after 2026. I don't know about you, but that is too close for comfort. One of the main prophets of this caliber is names Mother Shipton, finally killed as a witch, she tried to tell everyone what she saw, but people would not listen. Another was Nostradamus. In order to keep from being killed himself, his family name was changed to a Christina name and he wrote is prophecies out of order and with a mystical flare. Still another was the Apostle John who was able to foretell the future thousands of years from when he saw his visions. Before we get into these discussions of the future, let me first describe to you what it will be like under Mosel rule in America. Some seem to think we just pay a tax and live as if nothing else was happening. Unfortunately, that is not the case.

Christians Lives Under Moslem Control

Christians and Jews found out exactly how they must live in a Moslem region under Sharia Law, in the Pact of UMAR who ruled Syria between 634 and 644. Let me just make a list so you can see if this is how you want to live.

1. Must not build a monastery, church, or a sanctuary
2. Must not restore any place of worship that needs restoration
3. Must not allow a spy into a Muslims church or home
4. Must not or hide deceit against Muslims"
5. Must not imitate the Muslims' clothing or speech
6. Must not Ride on saddles
7. Must not collect weapons of any kind or carry these weapons
8. Must not Sell liquor
9. Must not Teach our children the Quran
10. Must not allow public Christian and other non-Muslim religious practice
11. Must not build crosses on the outside of our churches books fairways and markets
12. Must not sound the bells in our churches
13. Must not light torches in funeral processions that can be seen by Muslims
14. Must not Bury the dead next to Muslim dead
15. Must not buy servants who were captured by Muslims

16. Must not invite anyone to a church
17. Must not embrace Islam
18. Must not Beat any Muslim

Additionally, Christians had these thing they had to do is they did not want to be killed.

19. Must agree to pay a jizya tax
20. Must allow Muslims to rest "in our churches at any time desired.
21. Must open the doors of our homes to all Moslem passer-byes";
22. Must provide board and food for "those Muslims who come as guests" for three days;
23. Must move from the places we sit in if a Moslem chooses to sit in them"
24. Must have the front of our hair cut, wear our customary clothes wherever we are, wear belts around our waist" so that a Muslim recognizes a non-Muslim as such
25. Must be guides for Muslims and refrain from breaching their privacy in their homes."
26. If they were going on a roadway, they had to pull over to the side until a Moslem passed.

Muhammad also declared that the Christians and Jews cannot walk on the same road as the Muslim.

"Do not initiate the Salam [greeting of peace] to the Jews and Christians, and if you meet any of them in a road, <u>force them to its narrowest alley.</u>"

Shipton's Moslem War

First, let's look at this Mother Shipton character. Her real name was Ursula Sontheil and she is a reasonable prophet to use because of her accuracy. Her prophecies have had an extremely good record for coming true just like those of the more famous Nostradamus and Dr. Casey characters. Here is a short list of extremely detailed and accurately predicted historical elements that she wrote about. People thought that she was a witch and eventually killed her, but before they did, she had unveiled the future. [By the way, she accurately predicted the method and timing of her own lynching. I think it is better not knowing what the future will bring, sometimes.] She predicted the following:

- Automobiles,
- The rise of the Church of England,
- Radios, telephones, telegraphs, hydroelectric power,
- Manufacture of mountain tunnels,
- Submarines, airplanes, & iron ships,
- The California gold rush,
- World War I
- US Civil War and the French Revolution,
- Airborne military and their use,
- British and French alliance during the World War,
- The Allies and Communist block, and the cold war,
- The France to England underwater tunnel,
- Women would commonly wear pants and have short hair, [an unthinkable thing at the time]
- Commercial air travel,

- Assemblies would be put together with huge machines,
- The printing press and how it would change writing forever.

She indicated that some time soon after 2026 a comet would be seen across the sky and hit Europe. Following this horror, there would be confusion in the land and the Moslems would take use of this catastrophe. If you don't like knowing our future please quit reading and you will not be as disturbed.

Moslem War

War will follow with the work in the land of the Pagan and Turk [Indicates that the Turks will eventually follow the Moslem nations in this pre-Tribulation War. This will become clearer in other writings.]

Moslems Retreat

The lily [USA?] shall be moved against the seed of the lion [sign of Persia], and shall stand on one side of the country with a number of ships. [The lily comes to the rescue. The Moslem lion is beaten back by a nation with a strong Navy, possibly USA.]

The Last Anti Christ

Then shall be the Son of Man, having a fierce beast in his arms, whose Kingdom is the land of the moon, which is dreaded throughout the world. [The reference to the moon seems to be referencing involvement with others from outside the earth. The son of man in this verse is not a reference to God's son, but is the leader of the "Christian Nations". He has a secret alliance with this beast thing. By using this alliance, he begins to take power away from the Moslem horde. Apparently, this beast he has in his arms, we will find has to do with the Biblical "mark of the beast" that will BECOME dread throughout the world.]

The Beast Controls the World

<u>*With a number*</u> *[possibly 666] shall he [This "son of Man character"] pass many waters and shall come to the land of the lion [Persia], looking for help from the beast of his country* [Some group goes a great distance across the water, probably the USA, to fight the Moslem Lion. Unknown to them, they will be aided by the beast; what Nostradamus called the Prince of Hell.]

Please notice that, while the Beast takes control of the World after the Moslems are defeated, Mother Shipton saw that there was a new alliance with the Beast of Persia [whoever that will be].

From this 15th Century Prophet, let's now go back to one of the Biblical Prophets and look for a comparison.

John's Moslem War

The last chapter of our Bible holds another Prophecy that is very similar. This section starts after the Comet attack and the world is thrust into something called the pre-tribulation War.

The Beginning of the Pre-Tribulation War

Revelation 9:13-19-The sixth trumpet season- third of mankind will be killed [The beginning of the Pre-Tribulation War. We will look at this event separately. Notice that each time there is a huge world war John sees 1/3 of mankind being killed. We will get into this war in much more detail. It doesn't end in this season, but continues into the time of the final trump.]

Revelation 11:2 The holy city shall they tread under foot forty and two months. [As Mother Shipton alluded to and John continued to identify, someone will conquer Jerusalem and much of Europe for a time. The candidate that will begin to stand out is the Moslem nations. This possibly tells us how long Moslems will take control of Europe for approximately 3 ½ years.]

Revelation 11:3-5 And I will give power unto my two witnesses, and they shall prophesy a thousand two hundred and threescore days. And if any man will hurt them, fire proceedeth out of their mouth, and devoureth their enemies: [This seems to indicate that 2 leaders will push back the Moslems after another 3 ½ years of Moslem rule. If you remember, Mother Shipton identified these two guys as F.K.

and K.W. I don't care who they are if they really push back these aggressors quickly.]

Revelation Ten Horns

The Revelation prediction, on the other hand, has nothing to do with sequential rule. It simply indicates that 10 kingdoms will arise from the nation that takes control away from the Christian Church and is the 7th kingdom [7 heads]. These 10 kingdoms will combine to form 7 nations and then plan to do battle with the Christian world. Initially 3 of the ten nations hold out, but <u>finally they join the Moslem Army of and take over Europe.</u> As this is sequentially positioned after the initiation of wars on earth and a battle in heaven, I place its timing to be just before the Tribulation period. Let's see what the verses, actually say.

Moslems Take Control

<u>Revelation 12:3</u>- and behold a great red dragon, having seven heads and ten horns, <u>and seven crowns upon his heads</u>. [Note the difference between this first depiction and the one presented in chapter 13, below. This one has only 7 crowns while chapter thirteen indicates that that 3 more crowns were picked up, but both this Quran and the following one are depicting the same thing. It is a group of ten non-Christian nations going against the Christian nations of the world. From other texts, we can clearly see this is talking about the 10 Moslem nations.]

<u>Revelation 13:1</u> And I stood upon the sand of the sea, and saw a beast rise up out of the sea, having seven heads and ten horns, and upon his horns <u>ten crowns</u>, and upon his heads the name of blasphemy. [We will see that ten non-Christian nations will attack the Christian nations by sea, just as this Quran predicts and we will find confirmation in the writings of Nostradamus and others. The ten horns are of extreme importance as are the 7 crowns and 10 crowns.]

Revelation 13:7 *And it was given unto him [the Moslem nations] to make war with the saints, and to overcome them: and power was given him over all kindreds, and tongues, and nations. [The reason that the Moslem nations have been indicated as the aggressor will be much more evident in the section from Nostradamus and if you recall from the Mother Shipton section the aggressors were termed as those coming from Persia which would be the same group.*

Moslem Empire

The 7th kingdom as indicated above was that of the Moslem Empire. This, I believe, is significant and by using the details from the predictions of Nostradamus we can get a very good idea who six of the Moslem aggressor will be as they are called out directly in his work. We can guess about the others and we can guess who the hold out nations will be. Nostradamus calls out two of them as Turkey and Egypt. I would expect that the last one will be Saudi Arabia, but that is just a guess.

Called out by Nostradamus Iran **[Persia], Iraq [Babylon], Egypt, Turkey, Libya, and Saudi Arabia**

The other 4'groups" not called out by name- **Pakistan/ Afghanistan, Lebanon/Palestine/Syria [probably join with Turkey.], Kuwait [Probably joined to Iraq], and finally, Oman, UAE, Yemen, Qatar [probably join Saudi Arabia]**

The Moslem take control of Europe temporarily but are pushed back and that is where the "antichrist" comes in.

Mark of the Beast

According to both Nostradamus and Revelation, the Moslem nations don't keep control of the Christian nations, but instead a leader comes in and drives back the Moslems. Nostradamus claims this man to be of Germanic blood. One thing to know is that this new leader is a very bad guy. We can call him the antichrist, but that term is so used that its meaning is tainted. I like Nostradamus' term "Prince of Hell", because that is what he is like. This new leader is a bad man and institutes this 666 thing. Some references indicate two leaders jointly rule for a time, but the message is the same.

Revelation13:11 And I beheld another beast coming up out of the earth; and he had two horns like a lamb, and he spake as a dragon. [The tides turn and two nations, just like Mother Shipton indicated, take over the world, but according to John, these two nations only appear to be better than having Moslem rule. Soon the world is worse off.]

While all this 666 stuff is going on, let's switch to see what Nostradamus had to say.

Nostradamus' Moslem War

Michel de Nostradame lived during the end of the Inquisition and the new awakening with Tyndale and Knox. Still his family was from Jewish decent [originally Gassonet]. That could get you hung in France in 1500 so the Nostradamus family paid a lot of money to have their name changed to stay away from persecution. That being said, Nostradamus was writing his prophecies down about the same time as Mother Shipton. Neither one met, but both saw the same future.

Nostradamus gives us the most information by far. He not only details what happens he gives us the time in a star picture [as Venus, Mars, and the sun all are in Leo] The next time that happens is July 20th of 2014. My hope it is the next one. The main thing here is that we can gain a lot of information for this masterful prophet.

Comet Strike

Like John and Mother Shipton, Nostradamus saw a great European famine and plague that followed the comet strike. In its weakened state, Europe was ripe to be overrun and a Moslem Nation alliance soon takes advantage. This goes along the predictions in Revelation and other Biblical texts completely, but that is of little comfort. He even times the event as being in the 21st century.

[VIII-16] At the place where Jason had his ship built [Greece], there will be a flood so great and so sudden that one will have no place to fall upon. The waves of Olympian "Fesula" [Roman Island] will come. [The Comet strike will bring a tidal wave and that will be only the beginning.]

[II-96] A burning torch will be seen in the sky at night near the end and the beginning of the Rhone [southern France]; Famine, then sword, then relief provided too late. Persia turns to invade Macedonia [After the comet, there will be a terrible famine in Europe. The famine weakens Europe enough to allow the Moslem nations to strike Greece.]

[IX-91] The horrible plague will fall upon Perinthus [on the Turkey/Greece coast] and Nicopolis [Greece], the peninsula and Macedonia. It will devastate Thessaly and Amphipolis [both in Greece]. It is an unknown evil and from Anthony a refusal. [A plague also weakens the already weaken European nation. Possibly Moslems try to make a surrender deal, which is refused. That paves the way for war.]

During the third age, fire from the sky spreads from west to south toward the east, sterilizing the soil and leaving behind a country littered with glowing "carbuncles" and laid waste by famine. [More descriptions of the aftermath of the comet]

Even though Nostradamus' work does not provide us with a sequential timeline of events, his descriptions of events track the events brought out by John in "Revelation". Before this whole Moslem Christian war blows up, Nostradamus gives us information that could be vital in preserving what we can of humanity.

Moslems Take Over

Nostradamus continues with information about the terrible pre-tribulation war. The proponents of peace could not halt the onslaught of aggressors and war was on. By now, you know that he wrote weird, so you'll have to do some interpretation. He also wrote out of time sequence, but I'm sure you will get the picture. I put the sequential "quantran" number before each Quran and tried to place them in a more reasonable time sequence.

[I-40] *The false trumpet concealing the madness will bear Bzantium [Turkey] a change of laws. From Egypt one will go forth who wants withdrawal of the edicts altering money and standards. [Just like the Revelation prediction, the last trump signals in a great pre-tribulation war. Turkey and Egypt are reluctant, but go to the non-Christian faction]*

[V-25] **The Arab prince will come during the time of "Mars, Sun, and Venus in Leo" [next alignment will be July20 2014].** *The rule of the church will be succumbed by sea. [This indicates that the initial attacks are probably going to come from the Mediterranean Sea.]*

[VIII-96] *The barren Synagogue [Israel] will be without fruit. It will be taken over by the infidels.* **The daughter of the persecuted Babylon will be miserable and sad. Her wings will be clipped. [After the Moslem Nations Unite, Israel will be taken. {What a shock!}]**

[IV-58] *To swallow the burning sun in the throat, the Etruscan land [Italy] is washed with human blood. The chief uses a pail of water to lead his son away.* **A captive lady conducted into the Turkish land. [The Turks hit Italy while they are still riling from the famine.]**

[II-30] *One whom the infernal gods of Hannibal [Libya] relies will cause to be reborn, terror of mankind. In the past, no more horror or worse days are than will come to the Romans [Italy]* **through Babel [Iraq]. [The Iraqi will align with Libya, to take over Italy.]**

[III-60] Throughout all Asia [Asia Minor] there will be a great buildup of troops even in Mysia, Lycia, and Pamphilia [All in Turkey]. Blood will be shed because of the absolution of an evil young king filled with felony. [Again, we see a reluctance of Turkey to go with the non-Christians.]

[III-64] **The chief of Persia** [Iran] will engage great Olchades [Spain]. **The three-pronged fleet against the Mahometan [Mohamed] people comes from "Parthia [ancient Iran] and Media" [ancient Iran].** The Cyclades [Greek Islands] are pillaged and there is a long rest at the great Ionian port. [Greece] [Spain will fall along with Greece.]

[V-55] In the country of Arabia Felix [Saudi Arabian ruler?], there will be born one powerful in the law of Mahomet [Mohamed]. Buy sea, he will vex Spain, conquer Genada [Spain], and further, by sea, the Ligurian people [Italy]. [Possibly this guy is the "lily F.K." that Mother Shipton said would "lose his crown", and therewith be crowned the Son of Man K.W.]

[VI-80] Through Fez [Morocco], the realm will reach those of Europe. Their city ablaze and the blade will cut. The great one of Asia will come by land and sea with a great troop. Blue and Perses [dark blue] will come and will pursue the cross to the death. [Here come the blue turban thing we always here. If Morocco is taken, Europe better watch out.]

[VIII-6] Naples [Italy], Palermo [Spain], and all of Sicily will be uninhabited because of a Barbarian [non-Christian]. Corsica, Salerno, and the Island of Sardinia will find famine, plague, and war. The end of evil is remote. [The devastation is bad and the aftermath of famine and plague lasts a long time. Italy, Spain, and Sicily seem to be the hardest hit.]

[I-73] Because of negligence, France is assailed in 5 places. Tunis and Algiers [North African coast] are stirred up by the

Persians [Iran]. Leon, Seville, and Barcelona will fail leaving no fleet for the Venetians [Italy].

The graphic below shows how the invasion, apparently, proceeds.

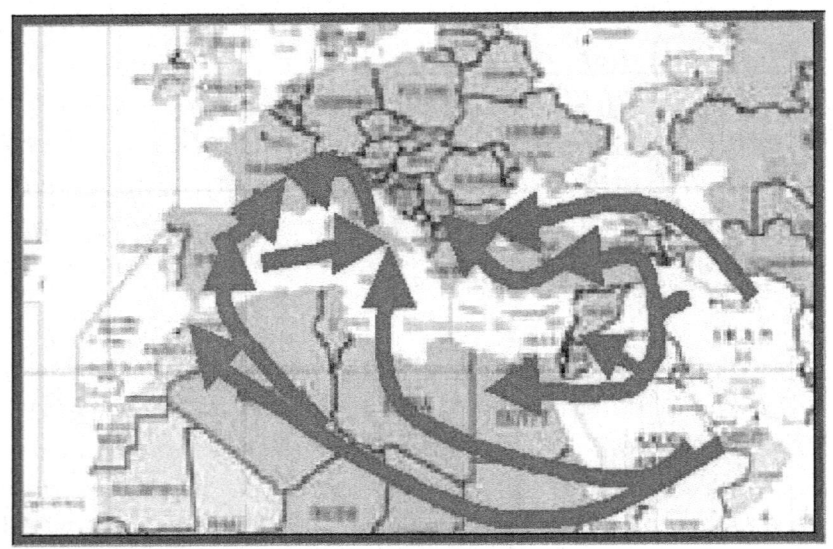

The Moslems are Pushed Back

These words speak for themselves. The Christian forces, initially from Russia and German, push the Moslem nations back, but it isn't easy and there seems to be reference to a nuclear attack.]

[X-75] *After time he will be pushed out of Europe. He will be sent back to Asia. As one of the League from the great Hermes [Greek messenger of the gods], he will grow over all the kings of the East. [Possibly this indicates that a mighty leader will come from Greece.]*

[V-27] *Through the fire and arms not far from the Black Sea, he will come from Persia [Iran] to occupy Trebizond [Turkey/Russia border]. Pharos [Egypt] and Mytilene [Greece] will tremble. The Sun will be joyful. The Adriatic*

Sea will be covered with Arab blood. *[This is clear, the Iranian Army tries to go into Russia and they don't make it. If that isn't clear enough, the next one says it again.]*

<u>On the fields of Media</u> *[Iran]*, Arabnia, and Armenia *[Russia/Turkey border]*, two great armies will assemble three times. The host near the banks of the Araxes *[border of Iran and Armenia]*, will fall in the land of the great Suleiman *[Turkey]*. *[Russians push back the Moslems.]*

<u>Towards Persia</u> very nearly a million men, the true serpent will invade Byzantium and Egypt. *[This portion of a Quran talks about the true serpent marching towards Persia, Turkey, and Egypt. This apparently predicts Moslems being pushed back by an even worse demon. As we found out from Revelation, this new serpent uses the number 666.]*

[V-16] <u>Flesh will be turned into ashes</u> through death, at the island of Pharos *[Egypt]*. They will be disrupted by the Crusaders *[Christians]* when <u>a harsh specter will appear</u> a Rhodes *[Greece]*. *[This harsh specter appears to be Nuclear.]*

[V-74] <u>A Germanic heart</u> will be born of Trojan blood *[Turkish?]*. He will rise to very high power. He will drive out the foreign Arabic people and return the Church to its pristine preeminence. *[This time it seems that the Germans are on the winning side of the battle lines and attack Italy. Also, note that the German leader, apparently, has descendants from Turkey.]*

<u>A final battle</u> just to the northeast of Salon leads to the collapse of Mesopotamian *[Iraqi]* power in France. *[Iraqi soldiers are pushed out of France.]*

<u>After tarrying, they will venture</u> into Epirus *[northwest Greece]*. The great relief will come towards Antioch *[Turkey]*. The black crimpled-haired king *[Moslem]* will run quickly towards the empire. The "Bronzebeard" will roast

him on a spit. *[After the "great relief" [possibly USA?] comes, the Moslems are quickly pushed out of Europe. The old "Bronzebeard" guy is not known to this author.]*

<u>*[IV-85] The great city of Tarsus [Turkey] will be destroyed by the Gauls [Germans]. All the turbans [Moslems] will be captives.*</u> *Help by sea will come from the great one of Portugal during the first summer, St. Urban's Day. [I don't know when St. Urban's Day is, but I suppose it will become a new Holiday of victory.]*

The graphic below shows how the Moslems, apparently, are pushed out of Europe.

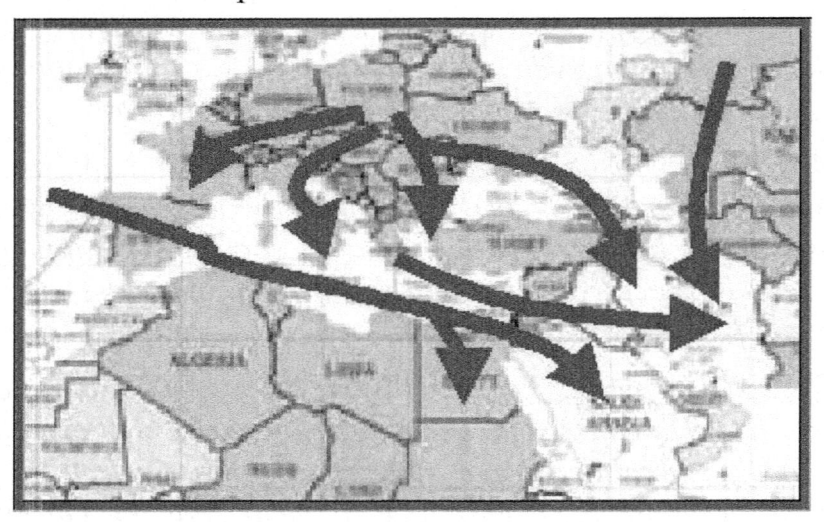

We have no details about how long the Moslems control the world, but we can believe is was for a long time as most conquerors control areas for at least 100 years. My guess is that most of the people of the world will know Arabic before the end of their reign.

Even after they are defeated, the person John called the Abomination of Desolation takes control of the world next, but that is a different story.

Ezra Moslem War

The 4th book of Ezra in the King James Version of the Bible is also known as the 2nd book of Estras. The prophecy in this book sound eerily familiar to those we saw with John, Nostradamus and Mother Shipton. This includes the Moslem take over and their eventual loss. Let's look. It gives us another confirmation of this bad time.

Plagues of Season Three

[15:11] I will smite Egypt with plagues, as before, and will destroy all its land." [As is indicated in other ancient Jewish texts, the Middle East destruction initiates this period.]

[15:13] Let the farmers that till the ground mourn, because their seed shall fail and their trees shall be ruined by blight and hail and by a terrible tempest.

Moslem War

[15:15] Nation shall rise up to fight against nation, with swords in their hands.

[15:19] A man shall have no pity upon his neighbors, but shall make an assault upon their houses with the sword, and plunder their goods, because of hunger for bread and because of great tribulation.

[15:29-33] The nations of the dragons of Arabia shall come out with many chariots, and from the day that they set out, their hissing shall spread over the earth.

The days are coming that the Earth will be under an empire more terrible than any before.

It will be ruled by 12 kings, one after another. The 2nd to come to the throne will have the longest reign of the 12. [I know Revelation indicated 10 nations take over the Christian world, but you could see from the previous list of Moslem states that it could be interpreted as more.]

After the 2nd king's rule, great conflicts will arise and will bring the empire into danger of falling, yet it will not fall then, but will be restored to its original strength. [The Moslem dominated kingdom will have some shaky times, but will not fall quickly.]

Eight trivial kings follow. Two will be left until the end itself. In the last years of the empire, the most high will bring to the throne 3 kings who will restore much of its strength and rule over the Earth more oppressively than any before. [Whether 2 kings, as indicated in Nostradamus and Mother Shipton's works, or three, as implied here, the Moslem's lose control and a new evil emerges worse than the previous rulers.]

Moslems are Driven Back

The Carmonians, raging in wrath, shall go forth the dragons, remembering their origin, shall become still stronger; and if they combine in great power and turn to pursue them. Then these [the dragons of Arabia] shall be disorganized and silenced by their power, and shall turn and flee. [It appears that the wars during this future time will be initiated by the Middle East and finally taken over by the Carmonians who have joined with many other nations. I chose to assume Carmonia means the USA, but that is just me.]

[15:34] Behold clouds from the east and from the north unto the south [South of Israel or the Arabs], and they are very horrible to look upon, full of wrath and storm. [The world is against the Arabs of the south.]

[15:35] They shall smite one upon another, and they shall smite down a great multitude of stars upon the earth, even their own star; [Seems to be referring to meteorite or flying ships of some kind]

[15:38] And, after that, heavy storm clouds shall be stirred up from the south, and from the north, and another part from the west. The tempest that was to cause destruction shall rise, to destroy all the earth and its inhabitants, and shall pour out upon every high and lofty place a terrible tempest. [The war is nothing compared to the "natural destructions."]

All the nations will leave their territories and unite in a countless host with a common intent, to wage war against God. Then, my son will destroy them without effort and with the lake of fire. [This is identical to the Nostradamus description and the Revelation description of the pre-tribulation War.]

After the time of famine everywhere, Alas for the world and its inhabitants! The sword that will destroy them is not far away. [Soon after the last Dark Age will be the war.]

Sibylline Oracles Moslem War

The Greek writers provided a great deal of confirmation and detail to our imminent future. The "Sibylline Oracles" is a long thesis written about 18 hundred years ago and covers many, many elements of our life. Some are not too well thought out. This one seems to be right on the money. Look for the similarities to assure yourself that these things are real and get prepared.

Comet Strike

2-235 His chariot celestial, and on earth arriving, shall to all the world display three evil signs [This seems to be talking about a comet strike, which is alluded to in many prophecies.]

2-245 A mighty stream of burning fire from heaven, and every place consume, earth, ocean vast, gleaming sea, and the heavenly sky; and heavenly lights shall break up into one and into outward form all-desolate. For stars from heaven shall fall into all seas. [The comet is predicted.]

Pre-Tribulation War

2-410-And desolations shall thy cities be and in the west there shall a star shine forth which they will call a comet, sign to men of the sword and of famine and of death, and murder of great [The falling comet signals the Moslem horde to the pre-tribulation war.]

Moslems Take Control

2-435 Of Asia, even thrice as many goods shall Asia back again from Rome receive, and her destructive outrage pay her back. As many as from Asia ever served a house of the Italians, twenty times as many Italians shall in Asia serve. [During the War, the Moslems imposed three times as much casualty and tribute as the earlier Roman Empire.]

Moslems are Pushed Back

2-483-In later generations into Asia's prosperous land shall come a man unheard of unjust, fiery; and this man wields the thunderbolt and all Asia shall sustain an evil yoke, and her soil shall drink much murder. [The Moslems are finally pushed out of Europe and the world is taken over by the "man of unheard of unjust", a man that Nostradamus called the Prince of Hell.]

Moslem Revelation

The Quran has a somewhat different prophecy concerning the years to come. In their prophecy, the Moslems taking over the world appear as an attempt to convert people to the truth while the pushing back of the Moslems is depicted only as the beast destroying the good. The section is known as "The Final Signs of Islam". This is the last prophecy of the book. It shows a different perspective, but it also shows a similarity.

Comet Strike

The ground will cave in: one in the east, one in the west, and one in Hejaz, Saudi Arabia. [It doesn't really say what is making the indentions, but from other works, it appears to be meteors.]

Pre-tribulation Dark Age

Fog or smoke will cover the skies for forty days. [This is the beginning of the pre-Tribulation Dark Age. The 40 days and 40 years continue to come up in these predictions.]

The nonbelievers will fall unconscious, while Muslims will be ill. [Plague predicted.]

The skies will then clear up. A night three nights long will follow the fog. Then the sun will rise in the west. [There is no mistaking this prediction. A major earth shift is clearly identified here.]

Moslems Take Control

People's repentance will not be accepted after this incident. [This could be a reference to the Moslem hordes trying to take over Europe.]

Antichrist Gains Acceptance

The Beast from the earth will miraculously emerge from Mount Safaa in Makkah, causing a split in the ground. [The beast emerges and pushes the Moslems back to Mount Safaa.]

Mark of the Beast

<u>The beast will be able to talk</u> to people and mark the faces of people, making the believers' faces glitter, and the nonbelievers' faces darkened. [The beast takes over the world and the mark of the beast is noted here.]

<u>A breeze from the south causes</u> sores in the armpits of Muslims, which they will die of as a result. [Another plague]

<u>The Ka'aba will be destroyed</u> by non-Muslim African group. Kufr will be rampant. Haj will be discontinued. The Quran will be lifted from the heart of the people, 30 years after the ruler Muquad's death. [The Moslems do not have a good position under the world rule of the beast.]

The fire will follow people to Syria, after which it will stop.

Tribulation

Some years after the fire, tribulation begins with the trumpet being blown. It will come upon the worst of creation. [The last Trumpet sounding and the Tribulation is similar to the Biblical prophecy.]

Conclusion

I'm scared. If you are not, you are simply living in a dream world filled with visions of happiness and splendor. ----or you are a nutcase.

America is losing control, Christian ideals are being taken away, Islamic populations are soaring, the required Jihad of the Islamic cult is on overdrive and the black flak of victory is flying everywhere. When Moslems kidnap into slavery thousands of Christina and non-Muslim boys and girls from schools simply because the school MIGHT be teaching western ways and we do nothing, shows that are losing the fight. When Benghazi weapon traders working for the Moslem Brotherhood are not tracked down after killing Americans, it seems we are losing the fight. When our President recites his poetry naming Jews the Apes of the earth, we had better think of someone new.

With That, I must close this book!

CPSIA information can be obtained at www.ICGtesting.com
Printed in the USA
LVOW04s0052140915

453988LV00021B/925/P

9 781500 124618